Sharing Your God Story

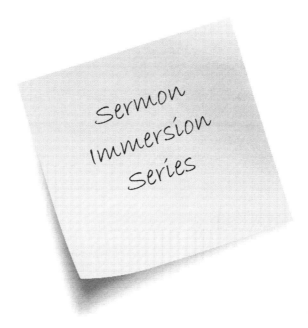

Sermon
Immersion
Series

Sharing Your God Story

Sermon Immersion Series:
Empowering Pastors and Small Group Leaders
Through Relational Evangelism

This book was designed to go hand in hand with
"Sharing Your God Story
7 Weeks of Empowering Devotionals
Designed to Help You Share Your God Story."

100% of the proceeds from this book series "SHARING YOUR GOD STORY" are being donated to "She Is Safe" whose good works "prevent, rescue and restore women and girls from abuse and exploitation in high risk places around the world, equipping them to build a life of freedom, faith and a strong future." *She is Safe* boasts of many God stories of how women and children were given new life through their work. For more information visit their website at
www.sheissafe.org

Sharing Your God Story
Sermon Immersion Series
Empowering Pastors and Small Group Leaders through Relational Evangelism

Rev. Dr. Sarah B. Dorrance
Middletown United Methodist Church
7108 Fern Circle
Middletown, Maryland 21769
https://www.sarahdorrance.com

Published by Dorrance-Babylon Media Group
Designed and coproduced by Leesa Ruderman Design, LMRudermandesign@comcast.net
Editing provided by Martha Lamborn
Copyright © 2017 by Sarah B. Dorrance. All rights reserved.
First Edition, November 2017

Acknowledgments
"Some Scripture quotations are from The ESV® Bible (The Holy Bible, English Standard Version®), copyright © 2001 by Crossway, a publishing ministry of Good News Publishers. Used by permission. All rights reserved."

Some Scripture quotations are from the Holy Bible, New International Version®, NIV®, Copyright © 1973, 1978, 1984, 2011 by Biblica, Inc.™ Used by permission of Zondervan. All rights reserved worldwide. www.zondervan.com The "NIV" and "New International Version" are trademarks registered in the United States Patent and Trademark Office by Biblica, Inc.™

Every attempt has been made to credit the sources of copyrighted material used in this book. If any such acknowledgement has been inadvertently omitted or miscredited, receipt of such information would be much appreciated.

ISBN-13: 978-0692955741 (Custom Universal) (Sarah B. Dorrance)
ISBN-10: 0692955747

FOREWORD

A GOD STORY

In the fall of 1996, my wife was pregnant with our second child. Our first child, Emily, had been an uncomplicated pregnancy. In fact, I remember my wife turning to me a few minutes after she had given birth to a girl, without the use of any drugs, and saying, "That's was fun. Let's have another." The second one was promising to be a little more challenging. There were signs of trouble, but I was not expecting the call at work that fall afternoon. "Meet me at the hospital. Something's wrong."

The placenta had torn. We needed specialists. They were able to stop the bleeding, but we were off to Johns Hopkins to understand what that meant for the mother and for the baby. I remember specifically praying for my wife. Not allowing God to be the big God that He is, I informed Him that He could take the life of my son if He spared the life of my wife (Insert "Lance is a big fat jerk" comments here). I guess that's how life has always worked for me. I expect God to fulfill my plan instead of trusting in His plan. I have an uncanny ability to know what's best for God and am not shy about informing Him of what He can and cannot do.

After a lot of pictures, tests, examinations, and stress, the doctor came into the room to talk to us. I can still see that examining room in my mind, etched there in fear and confusion. The doctor starting talking and pointing at pictures of my unborn son, pointing at spots in his brain, pointing at shades of gray and more gray and different gray colors of his kidneys and told us, somewhat matter-of-factly, that we needed to strongly consider an abortion. "Travis may have kidney problems, and he very likely has problems in his brain stem that will present as Down's Syndrome. Of course, it is your choice, but we would recommend that you abort this child."

I was probably in a state of shock. Time moved slowly as the doctor moved toward the door and I prepared to have the hardest conversation with my wife that I could ever have. Dawn and I would have to slowly go through all of the emotional pain associated with this decision. As the door closed and I turned to Dawn, I was shocked to see she was not in tears. Anyone that knows Dawn knows that she will cry at a good commercial for Rice Krispies and here she was, not in tears. I started to speak but before I could, she blurted out, "I'm starved. Can we stop at Taco Bell for a taco salad?" I started to ask her about what the doctor just said, and she looked me straight in the eye and said, "I'm having this baby." Dawn was immediately certain that Satan didn't want Travis but God did and he was going to have a special purpose on earth. There were many discussions after that, but the conclusion from Dawn, who listened to God, seemed far better than from Lance, who lectured God.

Every night of the pregnancy after that, I would go into my basement to pray for my son and my wife. And, I would play a song by Steven Curtis Chapman called "Hold on to Jesus." Every night I sang these words:

"I have come to this ocean
And the waves of fear are starting to grow
The doubts and questions are rising with the tide
So I'm clinging to the one sure thing I know
I will hold onto the hand of my Savior

And I will hold on with all my might

I will hold loosely to things that are fleeting

And hold onto Jesus, I will hold onto Jesus for life."

Before Travis was even here, he was teaching me to hold loosely to things that are fleeting and to hold on to Jesus for life. Our child was born with no health problems and now that he is the amazing young man that he is: athletic, kind, smart, and funny—he is still encouraging me to trust God's plan instead of my own.

And my wife? She is still teaching me who Jesus is. She is the greatest example to me of what it means to hold onto Jesus—and she gets Taco Bell whenever she wants. –Lance Barb

Lance Barb lives in Frederick, Maryland, and is a member of Brook Hill United Methodist Church.

PREFACE

SHARING YOUR GOD STORY

We love to tell stories. Narratives are how we pass information from one generation to the next—narratives are the way we explain what has happened in our family history—narratives are the way in which we communicate what is important in our lives. At every age, we tell stories. Yesterday a toddler told me the story about how she built a snowman in our deep snow. Many could see the joy that oozed out of this child as she told her very important story. A centenarian told me about the day they "no longer let her drive her car." Her freedom had been taken away from her. That, in turn, had caused her distress, so the narrative about no more driving continues to be her story every time I see her—for three years running.

Stories reveal every aspect of our lives—good times, sad times, funny times, and in-between times. Those narratives, however, are often missing something. Often the absent link from our narratives is God. Whether God was seemingly active or inactive is sometimes left out of our narrative stories altogether. Our culture is so afraid to speak of God outside of the church walls that we repeatedly leave God out of our conversations. Instead of asking the question, "Where was God in all of this?" we tend to remain silent.

Worse yet, we couch our responses in "culturally acceptable terms" such as, "Everything happens for a reason." Maybe that is fine for some people. For me, that is a very shallow response towards the God of the universe who created every living thing with intentionality and who invites every living human into a deep relationship with God's self.

Yet in our deepest pain, in our most terrifying moments, the first words out of our lips tend to be, "O God." We even read accounts of non-religious people calling upon Jesus at the last minute because that is what they have heard "religious" people say; and if there was ever a time to call upon Jesus, in our darkest moment might be just the right time.

Narratives tell who we are, where we have come from, and what we want to become. Our narratives are now being shaped in a different way in our technological culture. The internet has changed everything. Our narratives now come in the form of #instagram pictures; short sentences less than 140 characters for #twitter; and not really engaging our "friends" at all but stalking them on #facebook. It could be said that our means of communication is becoming more available but less profound. The new methods of communication are about abbreviation. Are we also abbreviating the great truths we have received? If we are talking about the most mundane of human activities this communication method might be acceptable, but if we are talking about what Jesus has done, we need time, and the new technologies are not adequate. They have crippled our ability to communicate deep meaning. Instead of having face-to-face conversations we are often reduced to a few e-mail communications. Even the time when we can just sit and be in the presence of friends has diminished, as we are often rushed to get to the next important thing. In today's culture we constantly observe families sitting in restaurants, each engaged with their electronic devices, but not with each other. Many of us fall into this trap of less human face-to-face engagement. Even as our face-to-face stories need to be more intentional, so does the inclusion of God in those conversations.

These next seven weeks are about how to enhance our God conversations. How do we live out a life narrative that shows that we belong to Jesus? How important is it to include God in those conversations? How do we address a post-Christian culture that often believes that church people are "judgmental and hypocritical?"[1] Do we want to live into that belief or do we want to convey something different? If we want to convey something different, what do we want our culture to understand about those of us who profess Jesus as our Lord and Savior? How will we live out that narrative in our lives? Jesus told us to love our neighbor as we love ourselves.[2] Will we be able to love our neighbor through our words, actions, and deeds? This study is about living out the narrative. It is my prayer that this study will empower you, through the power of the Holy Spirit, to get to the next level of sharing your personal God stories in your daily lives through your actions and your words. Know that I am praying for you, specifically I am praying that God will give you a holy boldness to be comfortable and even excited about sharing your God stories.

Thank you for taking the risk for seven weeks to see how God will empower you in sharing your own God stories. May our "life songs" sing to you, O LORD.

Many blessings,

Rev. Dr. Sarah B. Dorrance

Lead Pastor

Middletown United Methodist Church

A SPECIAL NOTE TO SMALL GROUP LEADERS

At the end of Lesson 7 the group is asked to think of a project in which they could have opportunities to share their God stories with someone they do not know. Please be working towards this project as you move forward through the lessons. Thank you for making yourselves available to be used by the God of the universe. -Rev. Dr. Sarah B. Dorrance

---

1 David Kinnaman. *Unchristian: What a New Generation Thinks About Christianity, and Why It Matters.* (Grand Rapids, MI, Baker Books Publishing, 2007). p.29-30.
2 Matthew 22:37-40, NIV.

ACKNOWLEDGMENTS

It is an honor and privilege to thank those who have walked this journey with me. Many thanks to the Taylorsville United Methodist Church saints for being willing to be the pilot teaching group for this study. I so appreciate your willingness to be there to try new things, to include this study. Thank you to the other four churches who were willing to be the ones to go into the unknown for a seven week sermon series: Brook Hill UMC, Middletown UMC, Deerpark UMC, and Wesley Grove UMC. Thank you for saying "yes." A special thanks to the Middletown UMC who received a new pastor, who then proceeded to preach this sermon series. You were willing to form small groups and come along.

The realization of this project in book form comes from another "God story." Leesa Ruderman, a member of the congregation that I currently serve, and I were hiking together one crisp summer morning. As we hiked we shared dreams and hopes for our futures. Our chat revealed that I hoped to publish this project, and that a publisher had promised to publish it six months ago and had not yet reviewed the material. Our discussion also revealed that she herself had the skills to type set this project and would be willing to take the project on if we were to publish it ourselves. What you are holding in your hands is the result of this "God Story." I am so grateful to Leesa for volunteering to work with me, to type set, proof, and for designing this beautiful cover. If you ever need a project completed, Leesa is your woman!

I'd also like to give a huge shout out and thank you to Martha Lamborn who was my patient editor throughout this writing process. Without her checking commas and quotations this project might have come to a complete halt. Thanks to Vieve McDonald who was willing to put data into a spreadsheet for me. Thanks to Debbie Beall who is my real-life, authentic, lay theologian. In season and out of season Debbie has a knack for being real and helped me translate this writing into something authentic. Thanks to my prayer partners for encouragement, specifically Debbie Beall, Teresa Martin, Carol Pennington, Susan Martin, and Lucinda Nelson. Thanks to Andy Cimbala who is always willing to talk theology with me in determining clarity of purpose. Thanks to all of my devotional writers, Rev. Dr. Wade Martin, Rev. Dr. Michelle Holmes Chaney, Andy and Melissa Cimbala, from Disciplemakers International staff, for last minute additions, Pastor Lynn Wilson, Rev. Dana Werts, and Rev. Sherri Comer-Cox. A special shout out to the faculty of Wesley Theological Seminary who encouraged me along the way, and my faculty reader, Rev. Dr. Douglas F. Powe. Dr. Powe, Dr. Wheeler, Dr. Birch, Dr. Weems, Dr. Parks, and Doug Strong, you are among my daily life heroes—I want to grow up to be like you. Thank you to my children Jamie and Melissa, and their God-fearing husbands, Phil and Andy. A huge shout out to the extended family, and especially my sisters, Marian Rognlien and Caroline Babylon, who patiently completed all the other family chores while I was busy writing. This project is dedicated to all of my family, my friends who steadily helped me through thick and thin, and to my Mother, Evelyn Fluck Babylon, who listens to my sermons every week, and was the first one to tell me God stories. Thank you all.

Many blessings,
Rev. Dr. Sarah B. Dorrance
Lead Pastor
Middletown United Methodist Church

INTRODUCTION

A LOST FIRE

Many congregations have lost their fire for sharing the gospel message. Many congregants have no clue how to share their faith. The reality is we are bad at sharing our God stories, and we are going from bad to worse. A God story is anytime we tell a short narrative of what God has done in our lives. Being able to articulate a God story leads up to being able to tell the greater story of the gospel message, which is what evangelism is all about—sharing what God has done for the redemption of the world. The fact that our Western culture has now been dubbed a "post-Christian"[3] culture should give us enough warning that people who call themselves Christians are not sharing their God stories. In mainline denominations in the United States church doors are closing, we are becoming more insular, and we are afraid to talk about God outside of our four walls. The post-Christian culture in the United States is hailed as such because we have professions of faith that are declining in mainline denominations, and churches are being closed more rapidly than new churches are being planted. Our story has to change. This project was designed to answer the question, "*How can we empower congregants to claim their faith story and to be comfortable in sharing that story so that they may share their story beyond church walls and others will come to know Jesus?*" This intervention was designed and executed to empower us to change the declining trend of professions of faith by learning to tell our God stories, and move towards being more comfortable in an evangelism narrative in a post-Christian culture.

GOD STORIES AS A BRIDGE TO EVANGELISM.

The word evangelism has long been a "dirty" word in our Christian circles. When folks hear the word "evangelism" they think of the person standing on the street crying out that we will go to Hell if we do not change our ways. We now hear the word "evangelism" used more in the secular world of marketing and football than we hear it in the church world. Yet, this word comes out of our heritage—and it is a good word. Theological thinker Len Sweet says, "The culture has stolen our 'church' words and the culture uses them better than we use them! Part of what we need to do is reclaim our own heritage and reinstate the healers, the peacemakers, the storytellers and the content providers in our congregations."[4]

People forget that this word "evangelism" is God's idea. They also forget that evangelism is relational. Christianity is about having a relationship with the God who created us, and who first loved us. That relationship is to be carried on between God and the created being, and between created beings. As we build relationship and trust with one another, we can grow to places where we can become more open to sharing our God stories so that these stories will have impact, and so that we can make the circle complete, and introduce others to the one who created them—and us.

We are all different in how God has shaped us and in the stories we tell. Evangelism uses words and action to tell our God stories. I have always been upset by the words that were supposedly attributed to Francis of Assisi, "Preach the gospel at all times. Use words if necessary." Yet, the research of Glen T. Stanton shows that this saying does not appear in any of Francis' writings.[5] The closest comes from his Rule of 1221, Chapter XII on how the Franciscans should practice their preaching: "No brother should preach contrary to the form and regulations of the holy Church nor unless he has been permitted by his minister... All the Friars... should preach by their deeds." Francis' first biographer, Thomas of Celeno,[6]

---

3 https://en.wikipedia.org/wiki/Postchristianity, accessed August 22, 2015.

4 Leonard Sweet. *Post-Modern Pilgrims: First Century Passion for the 21st Century World.* (TN, Broadman and Holman, 2000), p.42.

5 http://www.thegospelcoalition.org/article/factchecker-misquoting-francis-of-assisi, accessed September 18, 2015.

6 Ibid.

writing just three years after Francis' death, quotes him instructing his co-workers in the gospel as follows, "The preacher must first draw from secret prayers what he will later pour out in holy sermons; he must first grow hot within before he speaks words that are in themselves cold."

While there is a nice and good sentiment in "use words if necessary," the reality is that none of us can be counted Christians from our deeds alone. We all mess up. If people were following Christians just for our actions, then we would be a sorry mess. That might be the reality in which we are currently living—a world where we have failed to use words, and our actions have not been enough to pass along the gospel message. We need to learn to live into a "lifestyle of evangelism," a lifestyle of speaking and action!

RELATIONAL EVANGELISM.

Most people do not have a clue where to begin when we speak of evangelism, and they believe it is someone else's job. In addition, relationships in our culture have changed in how we interact with one another. Whereas neighbors used to be in relationship, now folks can live next door to each other and never know each other's name. In addition, the wealthier have gated communities, and the poor are sometimes afraid to go out onto the streets of crime-infested areas. Many homes do not even have porches or front doors from which to engage neighbors. Instead, many live with electric-powered garage doors. Neighbors may go a lifetime without seeing each other and without knowing each other's name. How do we build relationship with one another if we do not even know each other's name? How do we share Christ if we do not have a relationship with the nameless one next door?

Our reality is that evangelism is not even *ON* our congregant's radars! I am constantly reminding congregants that if their friends do not know where they worship, then they better do some more talking. This alone is counter-cultural. People no longer talk about their faith in public even if they do attend a church. When I grew up it was natural to know where all of your friends and enemies went to church. Now that rarely comes up in a secular conversation. How do we teach people to talk about this as a natural part of their conversations?

Helping people understand that it is the job of every Christian to share the good news of Jesus, and every Christian should have their own God story or testimony to share is difficult. It comes down to discipleship. How can we invite those for whom we offer services to participate and not just "do ministry" to them or at them? Evangelism is inviting people to participate in a changing society so that transformation can take place. As a pastor I am constantly trying to help people get to the next stage of discipleship. This takes time. The sharing of our God stories helps us grow in this discipleship.

It is my prayer that this immersion sermon series can empower others to learn how to share their God stories.

CONTENTS

Week One
Blessed to be a Blessing

SMALL GROUP LEADER - WEEK ONE

SHARING YOUR STORY - BLESSED TO BE A BLESSING

While the way that we tell our God narratives has changed, American Christianity has also changed the narrative of the church. The God story that we have heard in America has changed—in some ways, morphed, from that which was told by the early Christians. The resurrection of Christ had changed history. Literally, the lives of the disciples had changed due to the resurrection of Christ. They had seen how Jesus had changed the world, how Jesus had built community in order to usher in the kingdom of God.

They had been first hand witnesses of the work of Jesus. They had seen how Jesus had declared that, "The kingdom of God is near,"[7] and how the miracles that Jesus performed built up lives and changed communities. They had seen, first hand, Jesus ushering in the kingdom of God. They were eye witnesses to the cross and saw the place where sin and God met head-to-head. Yet, as scholar N. T. Wright has written, we in America have changed that early understanding of Jesus ushering in the kingdom of God. "Western Christianity has allowed itself to embrace [a type of] dualism whereby the ultimate destiny of God's people is heaven, seen as a place detached from earth, so that the aim of Christianity as a whole, and of conversion, justification, sanctification, and salvation, is seen in terms of leaving earth behind and going home to a place called heaven."[8] Yet, people are surprised to hear that, "The earliest Christians saw things differently. For the early Christians, the resurrection of Jesus launched God's new creation upon the world, beginning to fulfill the prayer Jesus taught his followers, that God's kingdom would come 'on earth as it is in heaven' (Matt. 6:10), and anticipating the 'new heavens and a new earth' (Isa. 65:17, 66:22; 2 Pet. 3:13; Rev. 21:1) promised by Isaiah and again in the New Testament."[9]

The earliest Christians were more interested in, "The final new creation, new heaven and new earth joined together, and the resurrection of the body that will create new human beings to live in that new world."[10] Wright goes on to say that, "This doesn't mean that we are called to build the kingdom by our own efforts, or even with the help of the Spirit. The final kingdom, when it comes, will be the free gift of God, a massive act of grace and new creation. But we are called to build *for* the kingdom. Like craftsmen working on a great cathedral, we have each been given instructions about the particular stone we are to spend our lives carving, without knowing or being able to guess where it will take its place within the grand design. We are assured, by Jesus' resurrection and the words of Paul, that at the launch of the new creation that the work we do is not in vain. That says it all."[11]

So here we are in this in-between place of dualism: one of looking at personal salvation and one of building God's kingdom now, which reflects God's heavenly kingdom here on earth. How do we live in the tension of both personal salvation and advancing the kingdom of God, which is the ultimate new creation?

One way we can participate in both is by sharing our God stories. Our God stories advance the plot of the kingdom of God on earth as it is in heaven. Our God stories share the good news of Jesus and help fulfill the mandate given by Jesus in the Great Commission. Ultimately, our God stories continue the biblical witness of sharing who God is and how God acts in the world—to a point of entering human

---

7 Matthew 4:17, NIV.
8 N. T. Wright, *Surprised by Scripture: Engaging Contemporary Issues*. (New York, New York, Harper One, 2014), p.84.
9 Ibid. p.84.
10 Ibid. p.84.
11 Ibid. p. 106.

history—in order to provide new opportunities for transformation in both this world and the world to come.

This is what Christians are called to do. We are called to advance the story. Yet, too often, we remain silent. We remain silent for many reasons. The list is long, but some of the main reasons for remaining silent tend to be: our attitude towards sharing the gospel message, our perceived ability, understanding the mandate given by Jesus, perceived opportunity, and a deep fear of offending or being reprimanded in work or public environments.[12] Some might even say that there is a form of soft persecution happening in our present culture to prevent us from sharing our God stories.

This seven week class is designed to empower us; to help advance our thinking; and to give us courage to share our God stories. We can only share our God stories, however, when we have the conviction that this is our particular biblical mandate. We can only share our God stories if we have encountered the living God; and we can only share our God stories if we know what we believe about heaven, hell, and the new creation.

For now, we are going to dig deeper into the biblical witness. The biblical witness from the beginning shows that this is God's story. God has invited us into God's story, by love. God did not have to create humans, but out of love for the world and all its inhabitants we were created. God's unfathomable love is the kind of love that has to share God's self, and results in a desire to fellowship with us. That is our model for sharing our faith. We share the God who deeply wanted to share God's self. It is kingdom work to speak of the King. God saw that God's created work was good, and God gives us opportunity to be witnesses to this story. A witness is one who testifies to the authenticity of a story. Ultimately, the word witness stems from the Greek word for martyr.

Initial creation was declared "good" by God. Humans were declared "very good."[13] This was the original shalom. This was the original harmony of the world. This was the original peace. This is the beginning of God's story. Interestingly enough, we also know the end of God's story—the one that stretches into eternity; the eternal time that we are told in the book of Revelation that the new heaven and earth became a reality—when the lion and the lamb will lie down together.[14] This is the ultimate restoration of that peace; that shalom—the way God intended it to be.[15]

We live in the between times. Those times of brokenness, those times when the world is not yet as God created it to be, those times—well, just look around you. Listen to the news, and perhaps you will agree that the world is not in relationship with God, with each other, or with all of creation the way God intended us to be.[16]

Sin entered the world through human disobedience and that which was good became broken—it became not as it was originally intended to be. Some theologians call this the doctrine of Total Depravity.[17] Others call it a sickness that needs to be healed. We can see that the New Creation is not here yet. We will get to the work of Jesus in a few chapters, but in the meantime, God did something through one family, one special family, whom God called the Israelites. God chose Abram and asked him to move out

---

12 James R Driscoll, *Sharing the Good News: A Workbook on Personal Evangelism*, D. Min Thesis, (Washington, D.C., 1996), p. 4

13 Genesis 1:31, NIV.

14 Isaiah 11:6, NIV.

15 Revelation 21:5, NIV.

16 Genesis 12:1-3, NIV.

17 This doctrine is closely linked with the doctrine of original sin as formalized by Augustine and advocated in many Protestant confessions of faith and catechisms, especially in Calvinism. The doctrine understands the Bible to teach that, as a consequence of the Fall of man, every person born into the world is morally corrupt, enslaved to sin and is, apart from the grace of God, utterly unable to choose to follow God or choose to turn to Christ in faith for salvation. Check out Ephesians 21:1-3. http://www.theopedia.com/Total_depravity, accessed March 31, 2015.

of his country, move away from his kinsmen in order to be a different people group. God promised to bless Abram, who was given a new name Abraham, but this promise was a two-way promise. This was a covenantal promise. Abraham would be blessed by God with both progeny and land. In return, Abraham's people were to be a blessing to the nations.

Too often we forget the second half of this covenant. Abraham is blessed, but not to keep the blessing for himself and his kinsmen. Abraham and his descendants are blessed *so that* they will be a blessing to the nations. Christians inherit the blessing of this promise through the grafting onto the vine of Jesus, but we also inherit the mandate, to be a blessing to the nations. Too often we want to *keep* the blessing and forget to *be* the blessing.

How do we become a blessing to the nations? One way is to share our God stories. Others cannot come to know the God of blessing, the God of transformation, the God of the new heaven and earth, if they have not heard the story. It is our job to tell the story.

As we continue in our journey together, it is my prayer that you will discover that this sharing of our story is not an option: that if we like the idea of sharing our God story we will do it, and if we are not comfortable with sharing our God story, well, we will just leave that part out. Rather, this is the responsibility of every Christian; to tell their God stories, over and over again, to all the people they meet.

Our stories should not be told by force or by manipulation, as has sometimes been the case, but rather our stories should be told in context of relationships. Relationships with the hearers provide an environment of trust, where the one hearing trusts us and trusts our stories. It means we are to develop relationships for the purpose of sharing our God stories. Sharing our God stories in the context of relationship is hard to do, but it is the way God wired us to be witnesses.

Where does faith come in when we tell our God stories? Abraham had faith in God to move his entire family to a foreign land to follow a promise. Do we have faith that God will be with us when we step out in faith to tell our God stories? What are we afraid of and what is the worst that could happen if our stories are not well received? The prophet Isaiah reminds us, "Do not fear!"[18]

Finally, where are you, right now, in your ability to tell your God story? It can be a small part of a God story. It can be a time when you were afraid, and suddenly the peace of God fell upon you in a supernatural way. It can be a time when you were trying to make a decision and suddenly, seemingly out of nowhere, something was said to you that you knew only God could have made happen. Ponder these questions as you go through the week. Please use the accompanying daily devotions to enhance your understanding that God has a plan for you, and you might be the only one who can speak spiritual life into someone in your circles of influence.

Before we continue, we have to know what we personally believe. This might not be something that you are ready to articulate today. Perhaps over the next seven weeks you can ponder these questions and write down your own responses.

---

18 Isaiah 41:10, NIV.

SMALL GROUP LEADER DISCUSSION - WEEK ONE

1. What do you believe about heaven and hell?

    a. Are the only ones who "go to heaven" the ones who have professed Jesus as their Lord and savior? This is a really important question for each of us.

    b. What about the nations who have never heard? Do we have a role in sharing with the nations? Check out Romans 10 for help.

        i. What does culture say about this?

        ii. What do other Christians say about this?

        iii. What does the Bible say about this?

        iv. What are your thoughts?

2. What do you believe about the New Creation?

    a. What should God's kingdom look like here on earth?

    b. Is there any chance earth as we know it will reflect the kingdom of heaven?

    c. What do we really mean when we pray, "Thy kingdom come" in the Lord's Prayer?

        i. What does culture say about this?

        ii. What do other Christians say about this?

        iii. What does the Bible say about this?

        iv. What are your thoughts?

3. Do you know what the gospel message is and how to articulate it?

    a. One possible place to begin is with Paul's words to the people of Corinth, "God made him [Jesus] who had no sin to be sin for us, so that in him we might become the righteousness of God."[19]

    b. Can you give an example of a restoration which reflects the gospel message in order to be a living witness to the power of God?

    c. How can you succinctly articulate the gospel message? (Remember, gospel literally means "Good News.")

        i. What does culture say about the gospel message?

        ii. What do other Christians say about the gospel message?

        iii. What does the Bible say about the Gospel message?

        iv. What are your thoughts?

---

19 2 Corinthians 5:21, NIV.

DAILY DEVOTIONALS - WEEK ONE

SHARING YOUR STORY - BLESSED TO BE A BLESSING

DAY 1   **WE LOVE TO TELL STORIES.**   **LUKE 1:1-4**

"Many have undertaken to draw up an account of the things that have been fulfilled among us, just as they were handed down to us by those who from the first were eyewitnesses and servants of the word. With this in mind, since I myself have carefully investigated everything from the beginning, I too decided to write an orderly account for you, most excellent Theophilus, so that you may know the certainty of the things you have been taught." NIV

My Mother is always telling stories of how she and her siblings went to her Grandmother's farm in Pennsylvania over the summer when she was growing up. I love to hear the story of the two seater out-house and how there was NO WAY she and her sister were going to use a side by side seating place in the out-house to do their private business. Stories make us laugh, stories make us cry, and stories carry down family traditions. We remember our family history through the sharing of the narrative story.

The same is true of our Christian story. Praise God that the gospel writer Luke was compelled to tell the story of Jesus. He gave us a narrative witness. Jesus was also always sharing stories. Many of them are called parables. You can probably even name some of them, "The parable of the Good Samaritan;" "The parable of the Sower." In reality the Bible is one great narrative, one great love story of how God loved God's created people. This truly is the greatest story ever told. The exciting part is that we are part of the story! We are part of God's story! As such, we have a role to continue sharing the story. We share stories of our families, why are we reluctant to tell stories of God's family?

As we enter into this seven week immersion series of "Sharing Our Stories," it is my prayer that you can be empowered by the Holy Spirit to think about your God story—and that you will have the courage to tell it. It has often been said that you might be the only person who will reflect Jesus to someone in your life. That person might be a family member, or that person might be a random person in the street that God placed in your path for a "Time such as this."[20]

As you become more keenly aware of your life story intertwining with God's greater narrative, you might also become more aware of places that are natural paths towards sharing part of your God story.

Reflection: How do you see God reshaping your story to be something that can be shared with others?

Prayer: God of all Creation: It is scary to think that I might be the only person reflecting Jesus in the life of someone else. It is even more scary to think that I might be the one to tell them a God story, a story of how you have encouraged me, and how that in turn, can encourage them. Empower me, through your Holy Spirit to have courage to speak when I do not want to speak. Empower me to listen, learn, and to be encouraged, just as others have encouraged me. Amen. -Rev. Dr. Sarah B. Dorrance

Notes:

---

20 Esther 4:14, NIV.

SHARING YOUR STORY - BLESSED TO BE A BLESSING

DAY 2 **WHO FIRST TOLD YOU ABOUT JESUS?** **MATTHEW 19:13-15**

"Then children were brought to him that he might lay his hands on them and pray. The disciples rebuked the people; but Jesus said, 'Let the children come to me, and do not hinder them; for to such belongs the kingdom of heaven.' And he laid his hands on them and went away." NIV

Who first told you about God? Who shared with you the Good News of Jesus? When my own children were growing up, some of our most precious moments were every evening when we read the Children's Bible together. I would even find my daughters, after lights were out, with a flashlight looking at the pictures in their Bibles. By the time they went to Sunday School at our local church they were already proficient in the stories of Jesus.

Many of us had stories of Jesus shared with us when we were young. Someone in your life probably shared a God story with you, too—either when you were young or as an adult. What did that look like for you? What do you remember from those times? Are those happy memories or sad memories? Perhaps today you can share one of those memories with someone.

What would you be missing in your life if that person or those persons had not shared God stories with you? Would there have been another place to hear the stories about Jesus? In 2004 the Barna study indicated that, "nearly half of all Americans who accept Jesus Christ as their savior do so before reaching the age of 13 (43%), and that 2 out of 3 born again Christians (64%) made that commitment to Christ before their 18th birthday. 1 out of 8 born again people (13%) made their profession of faith while 18 to 21 years old. Less than 1 out of every 4 born again Christians (23%) embraced Christ after their 21st birthday. Barna also noted that these figures are consistent with similar studies it has conducted during the past 20 years, saying that is easier to come to know Jesus when we are younger than when we are older.[21]

Reflection: Give thanks to God this day for those who shared God stories with you. What child can hear a God story from you?

Prayer: God, this day I give you thanks for those who told me about you. I thank you for those who cared about me enough to tell me about Jesus. Place on my heart today, those persons with whom I might be able to share Jesus. Give me wisdom to know when to speak, and wisdom to know when to be silent. Amen. -Rev. Dr. Sarah B. Dorrance

Notes:

---

21 https://www.barna.org/barna-update/article/5-barna-update/196-evangelism-is-most-effective-among-kids#.VQ9uT-GODMs, accessed March 22, 2015.

SHARING YOUR STORY - BLESSED TO BE A BLESSING

DAY 3   **BLESSING THE NATIONS.**   **GENESIS 26:4**

"I will make your descendants as numerous as the stars in the sky and will give them all these lands, and through your offspring all nations on earth will be blessed." NIV

God made a covenantal promise with Abraham. Abraham was blessed so that he would be a blessing to the nations. That promise went down through Abraham's descendants, always with the stipulation that they were to be a blessing to the other nations. That promise goes through all the descendants of Abraham, to Isaac and all the others, and ultimately the promise continues through Jesus and becomes grafted onto those who call themselves Christians.

Blessing the nations is another way of being our "brother's keeper." We see the effects of sin in the first offspring from Adam and Eve, when Cain killed his brother Abel. The question Cain asks of God is, "Am I my brother's keeper?"[22]

In our culture we continue to ask this question, "Am I my brother's keeper?" "Am I responsible for the nations?" The biblical witness from beginning to end seems to give us a resounding "yes." From Cain and Abel, to the promise given to the descendants of Abraham, to Jesus seeing that the people were like "sheep without a shepherd."[23] How did Jesus respond? Jesus had compassion upon the people. Jesus had compassion for the nations.

So how do we bless the nations? One way is that we are to be a godly reflection to them. We are to be so aligned with God that others want to know who God is because of our demeanor; because of our actions; because of the way we care for others; because of our communities; because of our hope; and because we are kingdom builders. How are we doing in blessing the nations?

Reflection: How can you be a blessing to those who are placed around you in your daily living?

Prayer: God, I fall short of your glory and I fall short of reflecting you in the world. Empower me to see the nations and our neighbors with your eyes. Remind me that you love each of them as much as you love me. Help me to be my brother's keeper. Amen. -Rev. Dr. Sarah B. Dorrance

Notes:

---

22 Genesis 4:9, NIV.
23 Matthew 9:36, NIV.

SHARING YOUR STORY - BLESSED TO BE A BLESSING

DAY 4   **THE GOSPEL MESSAGE.**   **2 CORINTHIANS 5:21**

"God made him who had no sin to be sin for us, so that in him we might become the righteousness of God." NIV

The signs in the stadium read, "We believe!" It was not hard to know what the people holding the signs believed in—this was the state championship high school football game. Everyone knew that the signs were an indicator that those around believed the team they supported could win the game. We believe! Christians should be holding those kinds of signs. "We believe!" One of the first problems the sign holder would have to face is, "In what or in whom do I believe?" Often times we have trouble articulating what we believe as Christians. We know some of the "fancy" words, but do we know what we believe? Do I know what I believe?

The Nicene Creed, written by the early church Bishops during the first Ecumenical Council in 325 A.D., is considered one of the universal documents to clarify what a Christian believes. In the Nicene Creed, we state the gospel message. What is the gospel message? That Jesus on the cross became the sin that every human has been and has done, so that the wrath of God for the effects of sin, would not fall upon humans, but rather on Jesus on the cross. Humans were, because of the work of Christ on the cross, made sinless and could be reconciled to God—in spite of sin. Sin can be defined as anything that separates us from God. If Jesus was in the football stadium and you were holding up a sign, what would that sign say? This is a good time to consider the question, "What do you believe?" The answer to that question might change over time, or it might have already changed. Our God stories become more powerful if we know what we believe about who God is and how God acts in the world. As the man stated in Mark 9:24, "Lord I do believe, help my unbelief." Be honest before God. Share your deepest longing, for God already knows your heart's desire. We can win the game too!

Reflection: Read the Nicene Creed. (https://www.ccel.org/creeds/nicene.creed.html.) Is there anything in this creed about which you are uncertain? If you have questions, ask your pastor or small group leader. Today is a good time to sit down and begin the process of thinking through what you believe.

Prayer: Father, Son, and Holy Spirit: This day I come before you begging for you to empower me to believe those things that might be more difficult for me to understand or articulate. Lord, I believe, help my unbelief. Amen. -Rev. Dr. Sarah B. Dorrance

Notes:

DAILY DEVOTONALS - WEEK ONE

SHARING YOUR STORY - BLESSED TO BE A BLESSING

DAY 5	BEAUTIFUL FEET.	ROMANS 10:14-15

"How, then, can they call on the one they have not believed in? And how can they believe in the one of whom they have not heard? And how can they hear without someone preaching to them? And how can anyone preach unless they are sent? As it is written: 'How beautiful are the feet of those who bring good news!'" NIV

When I was a child I would look at people's feet. I would often wonder where those feet had been and where they had carried the person. Where will those feet go next?

A greater understanding of the role of feet began to slowly dawn on me as I read the words of Paul, who was referring back to the prophet Isaiah, who says, "How beautiful on the mountains are the feet of those who bring good news, who proclaim peace, who bring good tidings, who proclaim salvation, who say to Zion, 'Your God reigns!'"[24]

If Paul had not taken the gospel message out to the nations, you and I might never have heard about Jesus. We might not have had the opportunity to hear the hope that is in Christ. It might be hard to believe in our technological age that there are still nations around the world and people groups who have not heard about Jesus. It is even more difficult to believe there are people in our own neighborhoods who have not heard the gospel message. Yet, there are people in our own backyards who, while they have driven past churches, really do not know what people "do" inside a church. To them, church is a place of judgment and condemnation of the world. To them, church is irrelevant to their lives.

You might ask, "How it is that people in our own backyards have not heard about Jesus and why are our churches perceived as irrelevant?" The reality is our American culture has changed. According to the Hartford Institute of Religion Research,[25] more than 40% of Americans "say" they go to church weekly. As it turns out, however, less than 20% are actually in church. In other words, more than 80% of Americans are finding more fulfilling things to do on weekends.[26]

As the map of American church life changes, so, too, we must change in order to meet the needs of the culture. Our message does not change, but the way in which we deliver the message and the way in which we reach American culture must change in order for us to be effective witnesses for Jesus.

This is where the missional church comes in. How can we bless the nations? How can we bless those in our backyards? This is our challenge. Are you up for it?

Reflection: How can you share the hope that you have in Christ to a people of a culture that might not see the church as relevant in their lives?

Prayer: Risen Christ, give me opportunities and the courage to be a reflection of you in my culture and in my circles of influence. By the power of your Spirit, help me have the right words to show that you are the only relevant thing in our lives. Amen. -Rev. Dr. Sarah B. Dorrance

Notes:

---

24 Isaiah 52:7, NIV.

25 http://www.hartfordinstitute.org, accessed April 12, 2015.

26 http://www.huffingtonpost.com/steve-mcswain/why-nobody-wants-to-go-to_b_4086016.html, accessed March 31, 2015.

SHARING YOUR STORY - BLESSED TO BE A BLESSING

DAY 6	HOARDING OR SHARING?	2 CORINTHIANS 9:13

"Because of the service by which you have proved yourselves, others will praise God for the obedience that accompanies your confession of the Gospel of Christ, and for your generosity in sharing with them and with everyone else." NIV

Sometimes my good friend in France sends me chocolates direct from France. They are some of the best chocolates of the world, and they are some of my favorite treats. Each time the chocolates arrive I have a choice to make: Do I want to share them with friends and family, or do I want to hoard them for myself? Sometimes our sharing of Christ is treated in a similar manner. It might not be that we are hoarding Christ, but we might not be sharing because we are afraid of what others might think, or we are afraid of being made fun of, or we just do not think it will be important, or we are afraid of retribution in our places of work. We have to find new ways around these roadblocks. Is knowing Jesus important to you? Then it might be important to another person.

The reality is that we have to do more than invite folks to weekend worship services. That is a good beginning. In addition, we need to find ways to build relationships, and we have to tell our own God stories. George Barna underscored some significant insights in his research. "Just as our nation's culture has changed dramatically in the last 30 years, so has the way in which people come to Christ," he explained. "The weekend church service is no longer the primary mechanism for salvation decisions; only one out of every ten believers who makes a decision to follow Christ does so in a church setting or service. On the other hand, personal relationships have become even more important in evangelism, with a majority of salvation decisions coming in direct response to an invitation given by a family member or friend."[27]

We have a choice to make. Too often, we do not consciously think of this as a choice, but rather we go about the business of our lives without offering hope in Jesus. Too often, like my chocolates, we want to hoard that hope for ourselves, or, we just do not understand the responsibility we have to share the Good News of Jesus with the nations.

Reflection: What makes you hesitant about speaking up about Jesus? Do you think this is important?

Prayer: God of All Creation: Empower me to be a sharer of blessings and not a hoarder. Sometimes I think I do not have enough, yet I know that you have blessed me to bless others. Help me to make choices that honor you. Amen. -Rev. Dr. Sarah B. Dorrance

Notes:

---

27 https://www.barna.org/barna-update/article/5-barna-update/196-evangelism-is-most-effective-among-kids#.VQ9uT-G0DMs, accessed March 22, 2015.

SHARING YOUR STORY - BLESSED TO BE A BLESSING

DAY 7   **KINGDOM BUILDERS!**   **PHILIPPIANS 1:27**

"Whatever happens, conduct yourselves in a manner worthy of the Gospel of Christ." NIV

A friend of mine had a good friend pass away too early in life. This 53 year old person had over 600 people show up at his funeral. Without fail, ever person attending the funeral said that the deceased had made a positive impact in their lives. That is kingdom building! Without exception, each person present said they were there because the deceased had lived a life worthy of the Gospel message.

The strange thing is, my friend never even knew he attended a church, she never knew he was a person of faith. When we live a life worthy of the Gospel message we are automatically building God's kingdom. We are making a difference in the lives of others without even realizing what we are doing. This has to do with how we love people. Are other people important to us? All of God's people are important to God. How do we love them? How do we care for each other?

There are times when we are moving so fast that we do not notice people around us or interact with them. Maybe we just interact automatically or out of routine. Does this sound like you in the grocery store or at the mall? There are other times when we are so absorbed with our own issues and problems that we do not pay attention to those who are helping us.

What would it take to slow down and observe what God is doing in God's kingdom? What would it take to be a kingdom builder and live a life worthy of the Gospel message?

Reflection: Are you a kingdom builder? What would empower you to be better at building the kingdom of God?

Prayer: God of the kingdom, I want to be a kingdom builder for you, however the very idea of sharing my faith story makes me very nervous. Give me courage to be your kingdom builder, and to live a life worthy of the Gospel message. Amen. -Rev. Dr. Sarah B. Dorrance

Notes:

SERMON OUTLINE - WEEK ONE

SHARING YOUR STORY - BLESSED TO BE A BLESSING

GENESIS 12:1-5 AND GALATIANS 3:7-9

1. Give a story [testimony] of when you, or someone you know, was a stranger in a foreign land. (For me, it was my junior year abroad in college, maybe it was your seminary immersion trip.)

    a. This time might have been a little scary.

    b. Took belief in many systems.

        i. The family system that had raised you.

        ii. Belief in God—that God would continue to be with you—faith

            1. Those systems helped make sense of life in a foreign land, in both good and bad times.

            2. It is hard to be a stranger in a foreign land.

2. Our biblical hero for today was also a stranger in a foreign land.

    a. He comes to us not only as a witness to God's faithfulness, but also as the Patriarch of the Israelites.

    b. He too became a stranger in a foreign land, just as I was, but this land would become the inheritance to Abraham's people, also known as the Israelites, and later known as the Jews. This land is the land of milk and honey promised to the descendants of Abraham.

        i. Even later, his descendants would become slaves in another foreign land, slaves in the land of Egypt.

        ii. But that is a story for another day.

    c. Abraham is the one spoken about in all the Jewish history books as the Father of the Israelites, the Patriarch, because he is the one to whom God gave this covenantal promise.

        i. He is a hero because he had faith to believe in the promises of God.

        ii. Throughout the biblical witness you will hear his name called out as a man of faith. As the Apostle Paul will say, "Abraham's faith was credited as righteousness." (Romans 4:9)

            1. So you don't get confused as to whom God was addressing, Abram's name was changed by God from Abram to Abraham.

            2. His wife's name was changed from Sarai to Sarah.

            3. These are the same people, with changed names.

    d. Abraham was the one who followed God's call to move to a foreign land.

    e. His descendants became strangers in a foreign land to pursue God's covenantal promise.

3. Here is a brief roadmap for the next seven weeks.

    a. Today we begin a sermon series entitled, "Sharing your God Stories."

    b. There will be several ways to connect with this immersion study.

        i. Church attendance for the sermons themselves

        ii. Small groups

iii. Daily devotional

c. We humans communicate by sharing our stories. Narratives are how we pass information from one generation to the next.

    i. Narratives are the way we explain what has happened in our family history.

    ii. Give a brief family narrative that is important to you.

d. Narratives are the way in which we communicate what is important in our lives. At every age, we tell stories.

    i. God has also revealed God's self to us through stories.

      1. The Bible is one big story about God's love for God's created people.

      2. The Bible is one big story about God's relationship with God's people.

      3. The Bible is one big story about God's community of faith, and how that faith is passed on to the next generation.

      4. The Bible is one big story of how God has redeemed (delivered; saved) God's people.

    ii. You have heard the story of God creating.

      1. God created the world and its inhabitants out of chaos. God's spoken word turned chaos into order.

      2. God's spoken word brought forth light and land and water and plants and animals and God saw that it was good.

      3. Then, on the sixth day, God created humans and said it was "very good."

        a. God walked in the garden with those first created humans and they enjoyed each other's company.

        b. But those humans were not puppets. They were created with free will and could make choices. They used those choices to turn away from God, to choose their own path.

          i. From that moment of disobedience, sin entered the world.

          ii. The created order was not as it was supposed to be anymore.

          iii. Sin and evil changed everything. God's people forgot about God, their creator. They forgot about their relationship with God.

          iv. From here forward God is pursuing God's people with God's love.

          v. God is calling God's people back into right relationship. God's people had turned away.

      4. So God begins to send missionaries into the world.

        a. Those missionaries are the ones who tell God's story, who tell a story of God's unfathomable love.

        b. Those missionaries tell the story of God's grace and mercy and forgiveness.

     5. As we move forward in this sermon series, we will look at how this sharing of God's story has unfolded throughout the biblical witness.

4. Here in Genesis, we see that God first chose Abraham to be the one to carry the story forward.

    a. Some would say this Israelite Father was the first missionary.

    b. Here is how it goes down.

        i. In order to speak to this world in the fullness of time, God *needed* a special people group, one that could be taught about God's ways; one that could learn about who God is and how God acts in the world. So God chose Abraham.

        ii. God *identifies* God's self to Abram.

        iii. God's election, or *choosing*, of Abraham and, subsequently the nation of Israel, concerns the whole world.

        iv. Why did God choose Abraham and his descendants? God chose in preparation for the complete unveiling and full disclosure of God's intentions for the world. God chose them to be *ambassadors to the nations*.

5. God did this through covenant.

    a. Covenant is more than a promise.

        i. Covenant is a two way street.

        ii. This is not just a promise, something said by the deity to an individual.

        iii. As theologian Bruce Birch writes, "This is a contract, rooted in the real-life economic, political and social transactions."[28]

        iv. "This covenant is a legal relationship, a legal oath."[29]

        v. Throughout the Genesis narrative, we see God challenging Abraham, "Walk before me faithfully and be blameless." (Genesis 17:1)

        vi. We are told that, "Abraham believed the LORD he was viewed as righteous by God." (15:6)

            1. Note that this is "LORD," which is the proper name for God. This is not just any deity.

            2. Note that righteousness included an attitude and a way of living in community and with neighbor.

        vii. So Abraham is going to receive a family, descendants, and land, and in exchange he and his offspring are to be a blessing to the nations.

            1. They are not just blessed to say, "look at me," but rather they are blessed to be a blessing.

            2. They are to bless the nations, not just their neighbors.

            3. All people are to be blessed through Abraham.

        viii. The blessing of all humans is to be through Abraham and his descendants, Abraham has a mission to fulfill.

6. As Christians, we are grafted onto Abraham's lineage through faith in Jesus Christ.

    a. Emphasize Galatians 3:7-9.

---

28 Bruce C. Birch, Walter Brueggemann, Terence E. Fretheim, & David L. Petterson. *A Theological Introduction Old Testament*. (Nashville, Abingdon Press, 1999) p. 78.

29 Ibid, p. 78

b. We become inheritors of the promise.

c. We also inherit the mandate, this contract of covenant, to be a blessing to the nations.

    i. You and I are to advance God's story.

    ii. We advance the story by being a blessing to the nations.

    iii. And here is the reality, we cannot advance the story and be a blessing, without knowing the story and sharing the story.

        1. We have to use words and actions.

            a. We live by example, and we tell the story.

            b. We share in community, and we tell God's story.

        2. And we are to share how our stories have intertwined with God's bigger story. Those are the best kinds of stories.

7. As we follow along for these next seven weeks, we are going to explore what it means to tell God's story in our own spheres of influence.

    a. Yes, you have a circle of influence, you might not realize this, but you have a group of people who trust you.

    b. You have built relationships, and those people listen to your stories.

    c. Do you share God stories with them?

8. Main point of this message:

    a. **God has a story to tell, and God calls us to share that story. God calls us to be a blessing to the nations.**

    b. Each of us is God's missionary.

    c. Each of us has been strategically placed, just like Abraham, to advance the story.

    d. Here is the sad part of this:

        i. We in America have abdicated our roles.

        ii. We in American churches have abdicated our roles.

            1. We have stopped sharing God's story. Don't believe me?

            2. Then why do we have fewer people who claim Christianity as their faith?

            3. Why do we have fewer people in our churches?

            4. Why do we have fewer and fewer of our neighbors who have stepped foot inside a church?

            5. Why do fewer people in our nation call Jesus their Lord and Savior?

9. The reality is we have stopped sharing our stories.

    a. There are many excuses: attitude, perceived ability, mandate, and opportunity are just a few of the excuses.

        i. Afraid of what others might think, not sure what to say, I don't want to intrude, not sure of how to tell this story, I just don't want to.

    ii.   Many people feel limits about talking about their faith at work, for fear of offending, or getting in trouble.

    iii.   Since the workplace is where we spend the majority of our time, and it is the place where we will meet more folks who need to hear the Good News, maybe this is another form of soft persecution. If we do not stand up for our rights to free speech, soon it might be real persecution.

10.   If there is anything we need to get right, it is this; sharing God's story.

    a.   All we have to do is look at nations that have gone before us.

        i.   Look at Europe, 5% of the population believes in Jesus.

        ii.   This is where our nation is headed.

        iii.   How do we reverse this?

            1.   By learning to tell our stories.

            2.   By sharing our faith in Jesus with others.

            3.   By building relationships with those around us and authentically sharing what God has done in our lives.

            4.   By being witnesses to what God has done.

            5.   I don't know about you, but God has done great things in my life.

                a.   Tell a brief testimony of what God has done in your life.

                b.   This is a resurrected life, a new creation from what I was, and I *do* want to share that with others.

                c.   You have a story to tell, too.

    b.   We are not all called to be preachers, we are not all called to be prophets, but we are all called to share our stories.

        i.   How does this apply to each of us today?

            1.   Maybe you are here today not sure you are even a Christian. That is fine, we are so glad you are here.

                a.   What would it look like for you to just be a blessing to someone? To do some random act of kindness?

                b.   Not sure how to do that? Make a blessing bag for those who are in need, put in useful items, keep it in your car, and when you see someone who needs a helping hand, give them one.

            2.   Maybe you are a Christian, but you feel that you have had so many heartaches of your own, or you have had so many health struggles of your own, that you have no possibility of sharing any story.

                a.   What would it look like to tell/share a God story to/with the very people who are helping you?

                b.   What would it look like to share a God story with your care givers?

            3.   Maybe you are here today, but none of your family is here. They are not sure why you go to that place called church.

      a.   What would it look like for you to be an extra blessing to them?

      b.   What would it look like if you were the one that blessed them time and time again?

   4.   Maybe you are here and you have no time, you are running your kids around and there is not even time to breathe.

      a.   What would it look like to share a God story with others who are struggling the way you are struggling?

      b.   What would it look like to share God stories in the car while you were transporting the kids to their events?

   5.   There are so many ways we can be a blessing to the nations.

      a.   Consider praying about it and thinking outside the box.

      b.   Consider asking God to give you opportunities, and do not worry, when you ask, God will honor that prayer.

  c.   Remember the story from the beginning of this message, when Abraham and his descendants were strangers in a foreign land? Even as strangers, God was still there, guiding, shaping, and molding.

11. Here is the reality. We live between the book of the Genesis beginning and The Revelation end of time. We know the beginning and the end of God's story.

  a.   In the beginning God created, and chose Abraham and his descendants, both biological descendants and grafted on descendants, to be a blessing to the nations.

  b.   In the end of God's story, the book of Revelation, we are told that, "The kingdoms of this world have become the kingdoms of our Lord and of His Christ, and He shall reign forever and ever (Rev. 11:15b). We are also told, "For all the nations shall come and worship before you. For your judgments have been manifested." (Rev.15:4)

  c.   We live in the between time and, as God's people, we are to advance the story, and bless the nations. For God will be known to all the nations.

  d.   How are we doing at that?

      i.   What role will you play?

      ii.   Are you willing to share your God stories in order to advance God's bigger story?

12. What role are you willing to play to build God's kingdom here on earth, as it is in heaven?

Amen.

LITURGY FOR WORSHIP - WEEK ONE

SHARING YOUR STORY - BLESSED TO BE A BLESSING

FIRST SCRIPTURE READING: GALATIANS 3:7-9

READING BEFORE THE SERMON: GENESIS 12:1-5A

CALL TO WORSHIP:
Come together as God's community to hear the story told.
Of Abraham who trusted God,
And his faith was counted to him as righteousness.
God promised Abraham land and more offspring than grains of sand,
And Abraham and his descendants were to bless the nations.
Come join the story,
Sing the song,
Abraham believed in the promises of God.
Come together as community, and trust God's promises,
As we retell the stories of God's faithfulness.
Come together as God's community, and celebrate what God has done!
For all the nations shall come and worship before you.

PRAYER OF CONFESSION:
God of the Nations, we confess that we often dream small dreams and think too narrowly. Too often we are only concerned about our own little world and we forget that we are to bless the nations, even as you have so richly blessed us. We pray for courage, we pray for opportunity, and we pray for your Holy Spirit to give us words and ability to share our blessings. Empower us to be your Easter people by embracing your story that intertwines with our story so that we can be building blocks in your kingdom. Thy kingdom come, Lord, as it is in heaven. Amen.

POSSIBLE HYMNS:
569 We've a Story to Tell to the Nations
567 Heralds of Christ
568 Christ for the World We Sing
571 Go, Make of All Disciples
572 Pass It On
123 El Shaddai
116 The God of Abraham Praise

* Page numbers listed above refer to the United Methodist Hymnal

POSSIBLE PRAISE SONGS:
Build Your Kingdom Here by Rend Collective
The Stand by Hillsong United
Go by Hillsong United
He Reigns by Newsboys

Week Two
God is Faithful

What is your story?

SMALL GROUP LEADER - WEEK TWO

SHARING YOUR STORY - GOD IS FAITHFUL

Do you believe that the God of covenant, the God who spoke to Abraham and his descendants, is faithful? Do you believe that God keeps God's promises? Can you give an example of God's faithfulness in the biblical witness?

The author of Psalm 86 proclaims the faithfulness of God with these words:

> *"Among the gods there is none like you, LORD;*
> *no deeds can compare with yours. All the nations you have made*
> *will come and worship before you. LORD; Teach me your way,*
> *LORD, that I may rely on your faithfulness; give me an*
> *undivided heart, that I may fear your name." Psalm 86: 8; 9; 11, NIV.*

How is the author's trust portrayed in these words? When you read the entire psalm, what do you see that the writer has to say about the nations? Read the entire psalm together as a class. Describe your feelings in reading these words.

If we believe that God is faithful, and if we believe that we are to be a blessing to the nations as described in chapter one, how can we bless the nations in our current churches and contexts? One way of determining how we can bless the nations is to see how God has been faithful in the past, so that we can remember how God will be faithful in the future. Two fancy words for this kind of remembering are *anamnesis* and *prolepsis*.

Anamnesis is bringing the past into the present. Liturgical teacher and preacher Larry Stookey reminds us that, "The present is but the thin moving edge separating past from future."[30] While we are fully in the present, the here and now, we grasp the past in one hand and embrace the future in the other hand. The past becomes remembered in the present through acting out what has transpired. This becomes a ritual process which we see in the Passover meal for the Jewish tradition and the Lord's Supper in the Christian tradition. This Greek word *anamnesis*, literally means "the drawing near of memory."[31]

In the same way we remember what God *will* do in the future through the Greek term *prolepsis*. This brings the future into our present reality. One way to define this is "to take something into our experience beforehand or ahead of the time at which it actually occurs."[32] We see this embodied in the Christian belief that the "resurrection is the entrance into the present of the future of God that is yet to be fully revealed."[33] The end of the Lord's Supper is a time when we remember what God has promised in the future. We also remember the future by saying, we do this until "we will feast at the heavenly banquet with Christ once again."[34]

We look at these two terms to see the faithfulness of God. It is the very nature of God to be faithful. Through the Exodus we are empowered to see how God was faithful to the people of Israel in their time of slavery. God delivered them in a powerful way. The people remember this great Exodus through the re-enactment of the Passover meal.

---

30 Lawrence Hull Stookey. *Calendar: Christ's Time for the Church.* (Nashville, TN, Abingdon Press, 1996), p. 28.
31 Stookey, p. 29.
32 Stookey, p. 32.
33 Ibid.
34 Liturgy used in worship for the Lord's Supper.

In the same way, we remember that God continued to be faithful in covenant by becoming flesh. The purpose of God *en*fleshed was literally to die in order to deal with sin in final victory. This is the way God chose to deal with the broken relationship caused by sin between God and God's people. We remember God's faithfulness of that life-giving event in the Lord's Supper when Jesus says this is the "cup of the new covenant, poured out by my blood."[35] We also remember the future that is to come when God promises to continue to be faithful until "we feast together at the heavenly banquet."

This is the God of covenant. That covenant was first made with Abraham, and it was carried down through his descendants. When Moses was called to lead the descendants of Abraham, the Israelites, out of slavery in Egypt, the covenant was renewed. "I will take you as my own people, and I will be your God. Then you will know that I am the LORD your God, who brought you out from under the yoke of the Egyptians."[36] Finally, the covenant was ratified at Mount Sinai. Moses brought the people out of Egypt to this wilderness mountain where God gave them the Ten Commandments. God became their God and they became God's people. Sinai represents the place where God taught the people how to live with each other in community and how to respect, honor, and fear God. This is the place where they were to learn how to be different from the surrounding nations, so that the nations would look to them and be astounded. God tells them that this is their purpose, "But for this purpose I have raised you up, to show you my power, so that my name may be proclaimed in all the earth."[37] Sinai was the place where the people learned to remember their past so that they could look towards the future promise—and they could know that God would be with them. The Israelites even had a huge sign that God was with them. They had a pillar of cloud by day and a pillar of fire by night to show that God was leading them, guiding them, and would not abandon them in the wilderness.

God knows we humans have short memories, so God reminded the people to teach their children about God. The *Shema* was repeated daily to remind them who this God was: "Hear, O Israel: The LORD our God, the LORD is one. Love the LORD your God with all your heart and with all your soul and with all your strength. These commandments that I give you today are to be on your hearts. Impress them on your children. Talk about them when you sit at home and when you walk along the road, when you lie down and when you get up. Tie them as symbols on your hands and bind them on your foreheads. Write them on the doorframes of your houses and on your gates."[38]

If we, the universal church are still God's covenantal people, as we inherit this covenant by being grafted onto the vine of Jesus Christ, how can we be faithful to the covenantal promise? One way is by blessing the nations. We bless them by being, what is often called, missional in nature. That means we stop looking inward and start looking outward to see how we can bless the people around us. The missional church looks outward to seek all people and to bless them. God has mercy on whom God wants to have mercy.[39] God uses the nations for God's greater purposes. God even tells the prophet Habakkuk that God plans to use a wicked nation to carry out God's greater plan. "Look at the nations and watch—and be utterly amazed."[40] If God can use the wicked to carry out God's plans, do you not think that those who are part of the covenant can do so much more for God's overall purposes?

---

35 Luke 22:20; 1 Corinthians 11:25, NIV.
36 Exodus 6:7, NIV.
37 Exodus 9:16, ESV.
38 Deuteronomy 6:4-9, NIV.
39 Exodus 33:19, NIV.
40 Habakkuk 1:5, NIV.

How can we intentionally look around us and seek out those whom we can bless? One way we can be missional is by building relationships with those whom we meet for the purpose of sharing our God stories. When we meet the people around us, we begin to get a sense of how our stories can be a monumental factor in blessing our neighbors, our cities, and the nations. Our God stories can help others connect to the living God. We become living witnesses to the God of covenant who is always faithful.

How can you remember your past for the purpose of building your future? Is there a way to remember what has happened in your family history to carry that tradition down through the ages? Sometimes we have to persevere through the tough times in order to even see if there is a future. When our times are difficult, it might not seem like there is anything at all for us in the future. These are the times to remember that God is faithful. If God has been with you in the past, what makes you think the God of covenant would let go of your future? This is the very reason we continue to turn to God, and, as Paul states, we "Throw off everything that hinders and the sin that so easily entangles. And let us run with perseverance the race marked out for us, fixing our eyes on Jesus, the pioneer and perfecter of faith."[41] And, we remember that God is faithful.

This is also where we learn to trust and obey the God of covenant who is not bound by time and space. God has a future for each of us. Can you envision what God might be calling you to do in the future? Can you envision a way to bless the nations?

---

41 Hebrews 12:1-2, NIV.

SMALL GROUP LEADER DISCUSSION - WEEK TWO

1. What biblical verse can be a mantra for your life, reminding you of God's faithfulness? (For example, a friend of mine repeats this verse as a prayer, over and over again, when she is going to her difficult place of work. "He [The Holy Spirit] who is in you [me] is greater than he who is in the world." (1 John 4:4, ESV.)

2. The people of the covenant repeated the *Shema* every day to remind them of God's character. What can you repeat every day to remind you of God's character?

3. God was present with the Israelites through a pillar of cloud by day and a pillar of fire by night. How do you know God is present with you?

4. What does it mean to be a covenantal people?

5. If we understand one of the characteristics of God to be faithfulness, what does God's faithfulness mean to us as individuals?
    a. As the church?
    b. As God's redeemed people?

6. Can you give an example of how God has been faithful to you in the past?

7. What are some other unchanging characteristics of God? (Hint: Exodus 3:7 is a good place to read about the God who sees, hears, knows, and comes down to rescue.)

8. If God has been faithful to you, how can you, in turn, be faithful to God?
    a. Can you give an example as individuals?
    b. As an extended family unit?
    c. As the church?

9. If you have extra time this week, listen to the song by Israel Houghton and the New Breed entitled, "More Than Enough." What thoughts come to mind when he says, "I'm living in the overflow?"

DAILY DEVOTIONALS - WEEK TWO

SHARING YOUR STORY - GOD IS FAITHFUL

DAY 1   **FOLLOW WHERE GOD LEADS.**   **JAMES 4:13-15**

"Now listen, you who say, 'Today or tomorrow we will go to this or that city, spend a year there, carry on business and make money.' Why, you do not even know what will happen tomorrow. What is your life? You are a mist that appears for a little while and then vanishes. Instead, you ought to say, 'If it is the Lord's will, we will live and do this or that.'" NIV

Do you wake up each day wondering what God has in store for you? I know I like to wake up, create my "To Do List," and be in control of my day, but God has taught me (and continues to teach me every day) that what I think I need to do and what God thinks I need to do can be remarkably different. Years ago, a colleague shared with me his morning prayer, he said, "I ask God to give me an open mind to be able to hear from God what I should do and with whom I should connect today." That simple prayer has stuck with me over the years and has become part of my prayer life as well. As a result I have encountered people and opportunities that I never had considered before.

Building the future offers us opportunities to witness to our faith every day. It is not hard. If we share our story and allow God to do the rest, amazing life-change can and will occur.

Reflection: Are you open to the leading of God and what God's plan is for you? Or do you go your own way, in your own power, remaining focused on what you hope to achieve?

Prayer: Gracious God, help me to place my "To Do List" in your hands. Give me the courage to share my story with others, to your glory not mine. In Christ Jesus I pray. Amen. –Rev. Dr. Wade Martin

Notes:

DAILY DEVOTIONALS - WEEK TWO

SHARING YOUR STORY - GOD IS FAITHFUL

DAY 2   **PERSERVERANCE.**   **1 TIMOTHY 6:11-12**

"But you, man of God, flee from all this, and pursue righteousness, godliness, faith, love, endurance and gentleness. Fight the good fight of the faith. Take hold of the eternal life to which you were called when you made your good confession in the presence of many witnesses." NIV

Sometimes our past or a part of our past is something we would like to forget. But our story is incomplete if we do not include the good, the bad, and the ugly. No one has a perfect past. We all have sinned, and thus have fallen short of the glory of God. This is why God sent God's Son Jesus to serve as the unblemished sacrifice for each of us who believe.

Because of this truth, as we receive Christ as our Lord and savior we can know with all assurance that sins are forgiven, past, present, and future. This assurance ought to give us the desire to persevere regardless of what we are going through. Even when things seem dire, persevere by holding on to the promise and truth of Scripture. The Apostle Paul tells us, "I can do all things through Him [Christ] who strengthens me."[42]

The ultimate end for our lives ought to be living as true disciples of Jesus, so much so we will follow Jesus through anything. We need to accept our past without regret and learn to lean into God's grace for the future. We need to quit beating ourselves up and allow the Holy Spirit to heal our hearts. As we build the future, God does not want us to focus on our past in an unhealthy way. Rather, God wants us to learn from our past, and then let God reconcile our past by redeeming it. "Fight the good fight,"[43] Paul says, and focus on the gift and reward of eternal life.

Reflection: Are there things from your past for which you need to seek forgiveness? Are you willing to turn any guilt and shame over to the Lord so that you can move forward to build a strong future?

Prayer: Almighty One, I know I have fallen short of your glory and ask to be forgiven. Use me, Lord, as your disciple to build a future focused on you. In your precious name I pray. Amen. –Rev. Dr. Wade Martin

Notes:

---

42 Philippians 4:13, ESV.
43 1 Timothy 6:12, NIV.

DAILY DEVOTIONALS - WEEK TWO

SHARING YOUR STORY - GOD IS FAITHFUL

DAY 3   **EMBRACE THE BASIC THINGS**   **1 CORINTHIANS 13:13**

"And now these three remain: faith, hope and love. But the greatest of these is love." NIV

Growing up, I really only knew one grandparent, my mother's mother. My father's parents died before I was born and my mother's father was an alcoholic who pretty much stuck to himself in the basement. My grandmother, whom I have come to admire over the years, was a woman of basic means. My grandmother never learned to drive and I am not sure she ever even wanted to learn. She grew most of her food in her large gardens, and she walked to the small store just up the hill from her house to get other needed items.

Whenever we would visit my grandmother, she always had a smile on her face and a kind word to say (even when we broke her flowers). When she worked in the garden she would hum her favorite hymns and talk to her flowers like they were friends. Of course as a young boy, I thought she was crazy. But as I look back on her life I have come to appreciate how my grandmother really appreciated the basic things in life. In reality, she embraced faith, hope, and love in all she said and did.

Conversely, many have made life today overly complicated and complex. We do not seem to appreciate the basic things as we once did. As a result we can tend to push God out of our lives easily. Other "more important" activities have taken priority away from our relationship with God: sports, sleeping in, work, and even family.

As we think about building the future, it all hinges on where we place God on our priority list. If God is not number one on our list, our future cannot be all that God wants it to be. We must embrace the basic things of life: "faith, hope, and love; and the greatest of these is love."[44]

Reflection: We are bombarded daily with things from this world that keep us from focusing on God. Do not allow your life to become unnecessarily complicated. Keep it basic and keep God first in your life. Live by faith, embrace hope, and witness to God's love.

Prayer: Lord God, have I managed to push you off the top of my list? Forgive me, and help me to return to the basics of life. Empower me to reprioritize what it is I give my attention to, so that you are number one. In Christ's name I pray. Amen. –Rev. Dr. Wade Martin

Notes:

---

44 1 Corinthians 13:13, NIV.

SHARING YOUR STORY - GOD IS FAITHFUL

DAY 4   **INSPIRATION.**   **HEBREWS 12:1-2**

"Therefore, since we are surrounded by such a great cloud of witnesses, let us throw off everything that hinders and the sin that so easily entangles. And let us run with perseverance the race marked out for us, fixing our eyes on Jesus, the pioneer and perfecter of faith. For the joy set before him he endured the cross, scorning its shame, and sat down at the right hand of the throne of God." NIV

As a pastor I have attended or officiated many funerals over the years. After some of the funerals I have said to myself, "I never knew that about the person" or, "I wish I had known them better." I get great inspiration from those who have lived the faith and have now gone on to be with the Lord. The stories of our ancestors can serve to inspire and encourage us as we navigate life's journeys to build a faithful future.

The Christian life is an endurance race, which includes many hills and valleys. But in the midst of this sometimes roller coaster ride, remembering the lives of those who have gone on before us can offer us inspiration and hope. The hope and promise of those who died in the faith is eternal salvation. Jesus opened the way to eternal salvation, and God's new Covenant will never be superseded. God creates our faith by God's grace through the Gospel and sacraments, and then the Holy Spirit brings us to the consummation of our salvation. As we cling to the memories of those who have gone on before us, may we build a better future so that all may come to know the saving grace of Jesus Christ.

Reflection: Are there people from your past who have died, yet continue to inspire you to this day? Are you living a life that can serve as an inspiration for those in your sphere of influence, or for those still to come?

Prayer: Lord, bring to my mind those individuals I know from my past who have had a tremendous impact on me. Remind me of how they lived so that I may be inspired to live a life that might inspire others. Amen. –Rev. Dr. Wade Martin

Notes:

DAILY DEVOTIONALS - WEEK TWO

SHARING YOUR STORY - GOD IS FAITHFUL

DAY 5   **ALL IN.**   **PHILIPPIANS 3:12-14**

"Not that I have already obtained all this, or have already arrived at my goal, but I press on to take hold of that for which Christ Jesus took hold of me. Brothers and sisters, I do not consider myself yet to have taken hold of it. But one thing I do: Forgetting what is behind and straining toward what is ahead, I press on toward the goal to win the prize for which God has called me heavenward in Christ Jesus." NIV

One of the attributes that keeps us connected to the saints of the past, present, and future is our willingness to be *all in* for the Lord. In Paul's encouraging word he speaks of *"Forgetting what lies behind and straining forward to what lies ahead."*[45] What this passage encourages is that Christians who go "all in" for the Lord, cultivate a discipline of:

- Focus on striving for the goal which Christ has set before us, until it is fulfilled, while not allowing the obstacles of this world to derail us.
- Making the decision to let go of past sins, and refusing to be paralyzed or rendered complacent by them.
- Following, by powerfully pursuing the calling of the Christian life, until the final victory has been won and the crown of glory is ours.

As powerful as the stories and witness of the past can be, we now have the opportunity to continue writing the story, a glorious story of Christ and Christ's relationship with us. Most of what is handed down to us comes from story, and many of these stories serve to encourage us to "press on toward the goal." As you consider your story, begin by going *all in* for the Lord and then allow your story to be counted among the many that will encourage generations to come.

Reflection: We all have a story, and it is part of God's greater story. How has or can your story encourage others? Have you truly gone *all in* for the Lord or do you walk around the fringes of faith?

Prayer: Holy God, I want to go *all in* for your son Jesus. Empower me to let go of those things that keep me on the fringes of faith and lead me to an *all in* relationship with Christ. It is in Christ's name I pray. Amen. –Rev. Dr. Wade Martin

Notes:

---

45 Philippians 3:13, NIV.

DAILY DEVOTIONALS - WEEK TWO

SHARING YOUR STORY - GOD IS FAITHFUL

DAY 6   **TRUST AND OBEY.**   **PSALM 84:11-12**

"For the LORD God is a sun and shield; the LORD bestows favor and honor; no good thing does he withhold from those whose walk is blameless. LORD Almighty, blessed is the one who trusts in you." NIV

Following Jesus into the future often requires recapturing the innocence of our childhood. When we were young, we accepted much of what we were taught at face value. And, in spite of a temper tantrum or two, we followed our parents and did what we were told to do, mostly without question. We had a level of trust in our parents.

As we march forward to building the future, we need to have that same level of trust, the trust of children, as we follow where God leads us, knowing that God will provide what we need and will show us the way forward. The first verse of the great hymn "Trust and Obey," written by John H. Sammis, puts it like this:

> *When we walk with the Lord in the light of His Word,*
> *What a glory He sheds on our way!*
> *While we do His good will, He abides with us still,*
> *And with all who will trust and obey.*

Reflection: Have you placed your whole trust in the Lord? What do you continue to hold on to that prevents you from giving your whole self to "trust and obey?"

Prayer: God of the past, present, and future. Create in me a heart of trust and obedience so that I might serve you. Remove any doubt I may have about your abilities. Give me a steadfast faith so that I may be the servant you have called me to be. In Jesus' name I pray. Amen. –Rev. Dr. Wade Martin

Notes:

DAILY DEVOTIONALS - WEEK TWO

SHARING YOUR STORY - GOD IS FAITHFUL

DAY 7   **VISION OF THE FUTURE.**   **PROVERBS 29:18**

"Where there is no vision, the people perish: but he that keepeth the law, happy is he." KJV

Jeremiah 29:11 reminds us that God has a purpose for each of us. The prophet writes, *"'For I know the plans I have, for you,' declares the LORD 'plans to prosper you and not to harm you, plans to give you hope and a future,'"*(NIV). What is your personal vision of the future based on God's purpose and calling on your life? As our Scripture reminds us, *"Without vision the people perish."* Without direction it is hard to know where we are going. When I speak, especially to young adults, it is disheartening to hear how many of them have no idea what they are going to do with their lives. When I ask about spiritual giftedness or God's calling on their lives, many give me a blank stare because they either do not know what I am talking about, or had not considered what God has gifted or called, them to do.

As disciples of Jesus Christ there is a call on our lives, a call that must be Spirit-led and Spirit-fed. A disciple's commitment is more than words, it is active, and it is a way of life. Like the prophets and saints who have gone on before us, disciples have heard the voice of God asking: *"Whom shall I send? And who will go for us?"* And they have boldly responded: *"Here I am—send me!"*[46]

Reflection: Have you heard or sensed the voice of God calling you (maybe nagging you) to go and do such and such? Have you turned away? What is your personal vision of your life? Is it in sync with your giftedness and God's call?

Prayer: Lord, there are some days I just feel like I am going through the motions with no clear vision of where I am headed. Through your Spirit, please give me clarity of heart and mind, so that I might see clearly where you are pointing me to go. In the name of Jesus the Christ I pray. Amen. –Rev. Dr. Wade Martin

Notes:

---

46 Isaiah 6:8, NIV.

SERMON OUTLINE - WEEK TWO

SHARING YOUR STORY - GOD IS FAITHFUL

1 CORINTHIANS 1:4-9; DEUTERONOMY 6:4-15; PSALM 86

1. Throughout history those who have tried to follow God have discovered this great truth...God is faithful.

   a. We read about God's faithfulness in the biblical witness.

   b. The Bible is full of stories from Old Testament to New Testament about God's faithfulness.

   c. Through the ages, those who have been leaders in the faith have done so because of the discovery that God is faithful.

      i. Some examples are: Martin Luther - storm, if you save me, I belong to you.

      ii. Or John Wesley, when he experienced the storm on the way to Georgia.

   d. But the reality is God is not a bargaining chip. We do not tell God that if God does this then we will do something in return.

      i. God is faithful in spite of what we do.

      ii. You probably have stories of the faithfulness of God as well.

2. We have been following Abraham and his descendants in the biblical witness, and today we come to week two of Sharing Your God Story,

   a. Last week we saw the covenantal promise given to Abraham.

   b. He was blessed with land and offspring, and in return he was to be a blessing to the nations.

      i. We saw him follow the promises of God by faith—those two words—"by faith" are really important—

      ii. It all boils down to following this God of covenant by faith, and that is where we make the discovery that God is faithful to God's promise.

3. Today we are looking more closely at this God of covenant.

   a. We are exploring the character of this God.

   b. We are known by our character—

      i. Oh, do you know that lady down the street, well yes, she is the one who smiles, or says hello.

      ii. Do you know the cranky person in the neighborhood?

      iii. Like it or not, we are known by our character.

4. The character of God is that God is faithful.

   a. Last week we saw the promise, and this week we see the reality of that promise. Indeed, Abraham was blessed with offspring, they did end up in the land of milk and honey.

   b. Then, through a series of events, beginning with the story of Joseph, the descendants of Abraham found themselves in Egypt.

      i. Once again, they were strangers in a foreign land, but this time they became enslaved there—enslaved in the land of Goshen, part of the Egyptian empire.

      ii. They thought the God of covenant had forgotten them.

    iii.   But God is faithful.

        1.   In Exodus 3 we hear the words, that God sees, hears, knows, and comes down to rescue.

        2.   Who is this God of rescue? It is the God of Abraham, the same one who gave the covenantal promise to this people group.

    iv. God used Moses to rescue the people, they leave the land of Egypt, to, once again, go the land of milk and honey.

        1.   God leads them in the wilderness to the place where the covenant is ratified.

        2.   Mount Sinai.

           a.   Sinai represents the ratification of the covenant.

           b.   Once again they proclaim God as their God.

The *Shema* is the way they proclaim their God, every day,

Hear O Israel, the LORD is one. Listen to the words: "Hear, O Israel: The LORD our God, the LORD is one. Love the LORD your God with all your heart and with all your soul and with all your strength. These commandments that I give you today are to be on your hearts. Impress them on your children. Talk about them when you sit at home and when you walk along the road, when you lie down and when you get up. Tie them as symbols on your hands and bind them on your foreheads. Write them on your door posts."

"When the LORD your God brings you into the land he swore to your fathers, to Abraham, Isaac and Jacob, to give you—a land with large, flourishing cities you did not build, houses filled with all kinds of good things you did not provide, wells you did not dig, and vineyards and olive groves you did not plant—then when you eat and are satisfied, be careful that you do not forget the LORD, who brought you out of Egypt, out of the land of slavery. Fear the LORD your God, serve him only and take your oaths in his name. Do not follow other gods, the gods of the peoples around you." (Deuteronomy 6: 4 - 14, NIV)

           c.

        God says, write it on your doorframes.

        i.   Story, my child really did write it on her doorframe.

        ii.   I could not get mad.

        iii.   She was following instructions.

5.   The Israelites wondered how they would know God was with them.

    a.   God provided a pillar of cloud by day.

    b.   And a cloud of fire by night.

        i.   Wouldn't it be great to know God is present through a pillar of cloud and fire?

        ii.   Yet there are ways we can know God is present, that God is with us.

6.   Here is an important part of today's message.

    a.   God is with us—even today.

    b. And the God of covenant is faithful, in every way.

    c. This is God's character, God cannot be unfaithful.

        i. In what ways have you experienced God's faithfulness?

        ii. Give a story of when God was faithful to you.

7. The Israelites experienced God's faithfulness through the deliverance from being enslaved.

    a. This is one of the pillars of their faith experience.

    b. They remember this deliverance through the Passover meal.

    c. How? By re-enacting it with their families that empowers them to remember.

    d. We know this God of deliverance too.

8. The God who delivered the Israelites from slavery in Egypt is the same God who continues to rescue and redeem.

    a. We remember that we have been redeemed by this God of covenant through the Easter story.

    b. God rescued us from the enslavement of sin through the death and resurrection of his Son, Jesus the Messiah.

    c. We remember the past - this act of redemption when we share the Lord's Supper.

        i. "Do this in remembrance of me."

        ii. And we remember the future: "Do this until we feast together at the heavenly banquet."

    d. We know God is faithful, and a God of redemption and rescue.

9. What does this faithful God require of us? Is there something required in return?

    a. Our return is not a barter system (as Martin Luther tried), but rather because God is faithful it becomes our desire to be faithful in return.

        i. Not out of works, but out of grace.

        ii. This is the God of free gifts of mercy.

        iii. What could I possible do in return for this God? The answer is that I can be faithful in return.

10. Last week we spoke about being inheritors of the covenantal promise.

    a. Jesus refers to this as the New Covenant, poured out by his blood.

    b. Part of our faithfulness, part of our returning the faithfulness, is that we are to continue being a blessing to the nations.

11. One way of being a blessing is to be missionally minded.

    a. Missional is when we think of those around us more than those inside the church walls.

    b. We learn to think outside the box to bless the nations (or our neighborhoods).

        i. We can be ready to share what that faithful God has done in our lives.

SERMON OUTLINE - WEEK TWO

  ii. We can learn to shift our story to be in line with a much bigger narrative, and it is the narrative of the kingdom.

12. Here is the main point.

  a. **We look to the past to see how God is faithful and we know that God will be faithful in the future.**

   i. Why? Because this is the character of God. It is against the very nature of God to not be faithful.

   ii. Now sometimes we might have different ideas of what faithfulness looks like.

  b. One way to remember how God is faithful is to keep the vision in front of us.

   i. In this church we have a vision of what we understand God is calling us to be.

   ii. Share your church vision statement. If you don't have one, use the UMC vision statement, "To Make Disciples for the Transformation of the World."

    1. The way we do this is by connecting with those around us.

    2. This is the reason that we do things like (share special events that connect to the outside world).

    3. Share a few more events that you have done to connect.

     a. We do this to connect with our unchurched neighbors.

     b. We do this to be agents of change in the neighborhood.

   iii. We have this vision, of being faithful to God, even as God has been faithful to this congregation.

   iv. We have this vision of being God's agents of change in the world.

   v. This vision is kingdom minded.

  c. As we live into the vision we also begin to understand that things might be done differently than had been done in the past, and that is fine.

13. How can we be a part of building God's kingdom?

  a. One way is by sharing our stories, right where we are in life.

  b. We continue to look to the past to see how God has been faithful in the past and will continue to be faithful in the future. We do this both as the body of Christ, as the church—the community of faith, and we do this as individuals.

   i. This is how we live into that dualism of being part of the new creation and understanding that this is the God of salvation.

   ii. We keep the vision in front of us. 1 Corinthians 1:18, "For the message of the cross is foolishness to those who are perishing, but to us who are being saved it is the power of God. And, therefore you do not lack any spiritual gift as you eagerly wait for our Lord Jesus Christ to be revealed. He will also keep you firm to the end, so that you will be blameless on the day of our Lord Jesus Christ. God is faithful, who has called you into fellowship with his Son, Jesus Christ our Lord." (NIV)

  c. God empowers us through the power of the Holy Spirit along the way.

   i. Empowers us to have courage.

      ii.   Empowers us to share our God stories.

14.   What has God done for you?

     a.   Maybe you are still waiting on the Lord, but perhaps you can find something pretty special when you search through your life.

     b.   Why has God chosen us and revealed himself to us?

        i.   I often ask that question.

       ii.   Share another story of God's faithfulness in your life.

     c.   These stories are designed to be shared, so that we can be that "city on the hill and let the light shine for all to see." (Matthew 5:14)

     d.   Your personal journey of faith is not just for you alone, it is part of the story of the cosmos. Your journey is one that is to be a story to be shared for others to come to know the God of covenant, this God who is faithful.

        i.   God reconciled the universe, and we are a part of that.

           1.   God has revealed God's self to us through God's faithfulness.

           2.   For me, there is nothing my heart desires more, than to be faithful in return.

15. What is your heart's desire in response to the faithfulness of God?

Amen.

LITURGY FOR WORSHIP - WEEK TWO

SHARING YOUR STORY - GOD IS FAITHFUL

FIRST SCRIPTURE READING: 1 CORINTHIANS 1:4-9

READING BEFORE THE SERMON: DEUTERONOMY 6:4-15

CALL TO WORSHIP:
(Based on Psalm 86:15)

Come together as God's community to hear the story told.
The story of the Lord God who is faithful,
The story of our God who is compassionate and gracious.
The story of our God who is slow to anger,
And abounding in love and faithfulness.
The story of this God who would go to any length to rescue his people,
The greatest love story ever told.
Come together, as we share the story of* God's *abounding love for us

PRAYER OF CONFESSION:
(Based on Deuteronomy 6)

Faithful God, we strive to be faithful, but we fall short of the mark. While you are faithful to us and call us into fellowship with your Risen Son, we often find ourselves pursuing those things that are not of you. Forgive us we pray. Impress upon us the importance of talking about you when we "sit at home and when we walk along the road, when we lie down and when we get up." Empower us to always remember our past, so that we can live into the future that you have set out before us. Amen.

POSSIBLE HYMNS:
710   Faith of Our Fathers
2172   We Are Called
698   God of the Ages
140   Great Is Thy Faithfulness
451   Be Thou My Vision

* *Three digit page numbers refer to the United Methodist Hymnal*
* *Four digit page numbers refer to The Faith We Sing Hymnal*

POSSIBLE PRAISE SONGS:
More Than Enough by Israel Houghton and the New Breed
Lifesong by Casting Crowns
Give Me Faith by Elevation Worship
My Lighthouse by Rend Collective
If We Are the Body by Casting Crowns
One Thing Remains by Jesus Culture
How He Loves by David Crowder
Your Love Never Fails by Jesus Culture
How Deep is the Father's Love for Us by Selah

Week Three
The Call of the Prophets

What is your story?

SHARING YOUR STORY - THE CALL OF THE PROPHETS

So far we have learned that the God of covenant calls us as modern day Christians into relationship with God's self, and we have learned that God desires to bless us, and God desires to bless the nations through us. This blessing of God is not for us to keep for our own selves, but rather we have a responsibility to share the blessing with others. We, as God's covenant people, inherited the covenant promise through the work of Jesus Christ, and we have a responsibility to *be* a blessing to others. The very reason why Israel and now Gentile believers have been named God's chosen people is so that we might be God's missionaries and witnesses in the world. Blessing comes with responsibility.

If you have a place to live, food on the table, and running water, you have been blessed. Give thanks to God, and ask God how you can share your blessing. The way United Methodists covenant together to be a blessing to the nations is through sharing our gifts of "prayers, presence, financial gifts, service and our witness."[47] How does your church or denomination make covenant together? This study is about renewing that covenant, with an emphasis on witness. Somewhere along the way we have forgotten that we are to be witnesses for God; we have forgotten how to tell our God stories.

But we are not the only ones who have forgotten how to tell our God stories. The nation of Israel also forgot how to share their God stories. They, too, forgot that they were to be a blessing to the nations. Furthermore, they had forgotten that they belonged to God. When things were going well and they were blessed, they kept the blessing for themselves and forgot all about the God who rescued them from slavery in Egypt. They forgot about this God of covenant, they forgot about their creator and redeemer. They forgot that they belonged to the God who is faithful. The book of Judges says that, "In those days there was no king in Israel. Everyone did what was right in his own eyes."[48] Everyone did what was right in their own eyes, this statement should sound very familiar to us in our culture of today.

God sent prophet after prophet to call the people to return to God. Throughout this period of history, often called the time of the kings of Judah and Israel, we see God raise up prophets to call the people back into right relationship with God. Each prophet reminds the people to return to the Lord. Each prophet reminds the people, through different means, that God is ready to receive them back as God's own people if they have a repentant heart and if they will choose this day whom they will serve. Jeremiah reminds them that God restores a faithless heart, Hosea reminds them to return to the Lord, and Joel reminds them that restoration is available to each of them for the asking.[49]

God uses Isaiah to remind them that a statue is no kind of God at all: "To whom then will you liken God, or what likeness compare with him? An idol! A craftsman casts it, and goldsmith overlays it with gold and casts for it silver chains. He who is too impoverished for an offering chooses wood that will not rot, he seeks out a skillful craftsman to set up an idol that will not move."[50] The prophet Isaiah reminds the people that God's word will not go out empty: "For as the rain and the snow come down from heaven and do not return there but water the earth, making it bring forth and sprout, giving seed to the sower and bread to the eater, so shall my *word* be that goes out from my mouth; it shall *not return to me empty*, but it shall accomplish that which I purpose, and shall succeed in the thing for which I sent it."[51] This is the

47 This covenant is renewed every time we receive a new member into the church and every time there is a profession of faith. See UMC Hymnal page 38. The UMC had totally forgotten to be witnesses in that the "witness" part was not even a part of the covenant until the 2008 General Conference, therefore, some hymnals might not be updated. See http://www.umc.org/news-and-media/united-methodists-will-pledge-to-witness, accessed April 23, 2015.

48 Judges 17:6 and Judges 21:25, ESV.

49 See week three daily devotionals.

50 Isaiah 40:18-20, ESV.

51 Isaiah 55:10-11, ESV.

God who is faithful proclaiming that God's word will not be empty, but will do what has been promised. What has been promised? The nations would hear of God's name and mighty works; that God cares about God's people; and that God's name will be known to the nations.

Some of the prophets began to tell the people that there will be consequences for their rebellion in not keeping God's covenant. In specific, Jeremiah states to the people that they should, "Stand at the crossroads and look; ask for the ancient paths, ask where the good way is, and walk in it, and you will find rest for your souls. But you said, 'We will not walk in it.'"[52] Israel chose not to walk in the ancient paths. The consequence of Israel's faithlessness was that God allowed another nation to conquer, to plunder, and to take captive Jerusalem and its inhabitants. This period is referred to as the time of exile. The people were in captivity. Once again they were strangers in a foreign land.

When in exile, God's prophets reminded the people to hold onto hope, and that something new was coming. The prophet Isaiah voiced that even in the midst of pain and suffering, God would allow them to, "Sing to the LORD a new song."[53] Jeremiah proclaimed, "Build houses and settle down; plant gardens and eat what [you] produce."[54] Jeremiah reminded them that God had not forgotten them, and that God was ready to do a new thing. God had not dismissed God's people, in fact Jeremiah proclaims, "For this is the covenant that I will make with the house of Israel after those days, declares the LORD: I will put my law within them, and I will write it on their hearts. And I will be their God, and they shall be my people."[55]

What about us in our day and time? Are we a rebellious people? Do we remain faithful to God's covenant? We, too, stand at a crossroads. Which path will we choose? What happens when we forget our own God stories?

In reality, we too, have not been faithful to the God who created us, redeemed us, and sustains us in this life and beyond. We have not been faithful in our, "prayers, presence, financial gifts, service and our witness." We stand at a crossroads and we have a choice to make. Will we choose the ancient path? Will we choose to be a blessing to the nations?

In specific, our churches have strayed from sharing God's story, and we have strayed from being invitational in nature. Instead of being a blessing to the nations, we have turned inward, worrying only about our buildings, our needs, and worship that pleases us. We have often forgotten that our worship is to give glory to the God of the universe, and not to be designed out of our own personal preferences. We have forgotten that we are to be the ones making our churches places where those who are absent would want to be, as opposed to making our churches places where *we* like to be. The church is not the building, but rather the church is the people who are called to be in right relationship with God and to share that blessing in our streets, in our neighborhoods, and in our cities. We have forgotten the missional nature of the people of the church, which is to bless our neighborhoods, our cities, and the nations.

The universal church is to be missional in nature. The design was never to be satisfied to sit in our churches and wait for the people to come. Rather, "The movement of the missional church seeks to rethink and redefine the nature of the church and create a new paradigm in which churches are seen as

52 Jeremiah 6:16, NIV.
53 Isaiah 42:10, ESV.
54 Jeremiah 29:5, NIV.
55 Jeremiah 31:33, ESV.

missional in nature, instead of attractional in nature. Leaders in the movement argue that instead of churches attempting to attract people to churches through church programs, churches should instead take the gospel outside of the church and engage society with the gospel, often by being involved in mission and evangelism (sharing our God stories). The missional church defines itself in terms of its mission — being *sent ones* who take the gospel to and incarnate the gospel within a specific cultural context."[56] The church has a missional vocation to reach beyond our structures and buildings to tell people about the God of the nations. Part of our covenant with God is to be witnesses, to tell our God stories, to be the ones who proclaim to the nations that there is a God, and that God has redeemed them through the life, death, and resurrection of Jesus, and that God is faithful.

Sing to the Lord a new song! The message of the gospel is the same, but the way we carry that story into the world has changed. We can no longer count on the unchurched just showing up at our church doors through an attractional model. That model is not working! Rather, we begin to share who God is as we come into relationships with our unchurched neighbors. As we build those relationships, those who are currently outside of the church will slowly join in as we serve in the world together.

The reality is that we are standing at a crossroads of culture. Christians are the aliens. We are the folks who do not belong to this culture. Yet we "Have been called out of the darkness to live into his marvelous light!"[57] How are we going to reach the nations for God if we cannot meet the culture where it is? What should we do differently? How will we reach our neighbors who have never heard the gospel message? What is the prophet calling *us* to do in our day and time? Maybe God is calling us to be the prophets!

In the year of 2015, the population of the Millennial generation surpassed the population of the Baby Boomers. Immigrants have expanded the ranks of the Millennials.[58] How are we going to reach this generation for God? Our current young people are looking for something that is spiritual in nature, but they have not found that something in our churches. Rather they have found our churches cold, unfriendly, and a waste of their time. They are looking for something authentic, real, and something that makes a difference in their lives. Those who know Jesus know that Jesus is the answer, but the way we convey the answer needs to change. One way we can change this paradigm is by sharing our God stories in our schools, in our workplaces, in our homes, and in our neighborhoods. Are you willing to share your God story in an authentic way with someone with whom you have built a relationship for the very purpose of sharing your God stories? Pray about it—see where God is calling you.

---

56 http://en.wikipedia.org/wiki/Missional_living, accessed April 23, 2015.

57 2 Peter 1:9, NIV.

58 http://www.pewresearch.org/fact-tank/2015/01/16/this-year-millennials-will-overtake-baby-boomers/, accessed April 23, 2015.

SMALL GROUP LEADER DISCUSSION - WEEK THREE

1. Have you ever understood God to be calling you back to right relationship?

    a. Describe that time.

    b. Is that part of a God story that you could share?

2. Do we see people in our day doing "what is right in their own eyes" like the Israelites?

    a. What was the standard for the Israelites?

    b. What is our standard?

    c. By doing "what is right in our own eyes" what are we forgetting to do? (We are forgetting to point to God.)

3. Check out this article about the Millennials that have now surpassed the Baby Boomers. http://www.pewresearch.org/fact-tank/2015/01/16/this-year-millennials-will-overtake-baby-boomers/ Most Millennials are not in a relationship with the church. Many choose to check "none" on a form when they are asked their religious preferences. What are your thoughts? How can Christians change the trend?

4. If you are part of a UMC, how do you live out your covenant of sharing your gifts through "prayers, presence, financial gifts, service and your witness?"

5. Do you know how to tell your God story or stories?

    a. Can you articulate your God story and tell it succinctly?

    b. Can you break down your God story into little parts? For example: this is a time I was far away from God; or I had surgery, and this is how I felt the presence of God; or I was about to lose my job but God provided peace in the midst of turmoil.

    c. Can you tell your God story in a way that people would want to listen?

        i. Can you tell a two minute version of your God story?

        ii. Can you tell a five minute version of your God story?

        iii. Can you think of someone in your circles of influence with whom you can build an authentic relationship for the very purpose of sharing your God story?

DAILY DEVOTIONALS - WEEK THREE

SHARING YOUR STORY - THE CALL OF THE PROPHETS

DAY 1   **CHOOSE THIS DAY WHOM YOU WILL SERVE.**   **JOSHUA 24:14-15**

"Now fear the LORD and serve him with all faithfulness. Throw away the gods your ancestors worshiped beyond the Euphrates River and in Egypt, and serve the LORD, But if serving the LORD seems undesirable to you, then choose for yourselves this day whom you will serve, whether the gods your ancestors served beyond the Euphrates, or the gods of the Amorites, in whose land you are living. But as for me and my household, we will serve the LORD." NIV

Joshua had just led the Israelites into the Promised Land. The baton of leadership had been handed from Moses to Joshua. The Israelites arrived in the land of milk and honey. Joshua was reminding them, once again, of God's covenant. He said they had to choose whom they were going to serve, for there were many distractions in the Promised Land.

It is no different for us. There are many distractions in our world as well. There are many things that try to draw us away from the living God; there are many things that try to pull us away from our creator, redeemer, and sustainer of life. Every day, we too, must choose whom we will serve.

When we do not stay focused on whom we are serving, we miss opportunities. Sometimes we not only miss opportunities, but we also do our own form of rebellion against God. Our rebellion can be a huge deterrent when we are trying to reflect God to the neighborhood and the nations.

Whom do you choose to serve? How will you live out that service on a daily basis? Is serving the LORD reflected in your daily speech and actions? Are you a child of the covenantal promise?

Reflection: In looking back at the past week, did you reflect God in your actions and words?

Prayer: God, I want to be a child of the covenant. I want to be serving you and sharing your stories. Too often I am distracted by the world around me that attempts to draw me away from you. By the power of your Holy Spirit, keep me steadfastly in relationship with you. Amen. -Rev. Dr. Sarah B. Dorrance

Notes:

SHARING YOUR STORY - THE CALL OF THE PROPHETS

DAY 2   **GOD HEALS FAITHLESSNESS.**   **JEREMIAH 3:22**

"Return, O faithless sons, I will heal your faithlessness." ESV

Have you ever realized you've been unfaithful to God? Maybe it's a missed gospel opportunity. Maybe you spoke harsh words to your family. Maybe you skipped your Bible reading to work on your hobby. The harder we examine our hearts, the more we realize that we just do not have what it takes. We are a bad friend to God. We commit to things then back out. We say we will attend to something then we do not show. We claim we will change, then we jump right back into our old habits.

God knows that we are faithless, we are not fooling God. But this is where God shines. God calls us to return to God's self, but not for discipline! This is not for a tongue lashing. No, our God beckons to us to return so that God can heal our faithlessness. God is the source of the healing that we desperately need. Earlier, in Jeremiah 3:12, God says, "Return, faithless Israel, I will not look upon you in anger. For I am gracious, I will not be angry forever." God calls us to repentance, but God does so through God's marvelous grace.

Reflection: How have you been unfaithful to God this week? Confess that to God now. What is God's attitude towards you when you are unfaithful? Answer: gracious. Take a few minutes to thank God for God's mercy and faithfulness to you.

Prayer: Dear Lord, thank you for responding to my rebellion with grace. Thank you for offering me healing. I need it. Please heal my faithlessness, and "bind my wandering heart to Thee."[59] Amen. –Andy Cimbala

Notes:

---

59 Quote from the hymn, "Come Thou Fount of Every Blessing".

DAILY DEVOTIONALS - WEEK THREE

SHARING YOUR STORY - THE CALL OF THE PROPHETS

DAY 3   **RETURN TO THE LORD.**   **HOSEA 3:1-5**

"And the LORD said to me, 'Go again, love a woman who is loved by another man and is an adulteress, even as the LORD loves the children of Israel, though they turn to other gods and love cakes of raisins.' So I bought her for fifteen shekels of silver and a homer and a lethech of barley. And I said to her, 'You must dwell as mine for many days. You shall not play the whore, or belong to another man; so will I also be to you.' For the children of Israel shall dwell many days without king or prince, without sacrifice or pillar, without ephod or household gods. Afterward the children of Israel shall return and seek the LORD their God, and David their king, and they shall come in fear to the LORD and to his goodness in the latter days."
ESV

The story of Hosea is a strange romantic comedy. In chapter 1 God calls Hosea the prophet to marry a prostitute named Gomer, to symbolize the faithfulness of God as the husband to Israel, his unfaithful wife. A few verses later Gomer is already cheating on Hosea, and his heart is broken. By chapter 3, she is being sold into slavery by her adulterous lovers, and God calls Hosea to do something radical: *go buy back your wife.*

This is a living parable of God's pursuing mercy and faithfulness to God's people! Even though we continually stray from God and disobey God's commandments, and run after idols, God still pursues us in God's faithful love. God promises in Hosea 2:14, "Therefore, behold, I will allure her, bring her into the wilderness, and speak kindly to her." We see this again in 2:20, "And I will betroth you to me in faithfulness. Then you will know the LORD." Our rebellion and adultery do not stop God's love. God stays true to us, even ransoming God's own life in order to buy us back out of our slavery to sin and death. We see this fulfilled in Christ, who paid the penalty we deserved on the cross, to rescue us as his bride.

Reflection: How have you betrayed the covenant with God? Of what idolatries are you guilty? God does not reject you, rather God is still pursuing you. Press on to know the Lord, and trust that our God is like a forgiving spouse who longs to have you back. God still loves you!

Prayer: God, thank you for your faithful love. Thank you for pursuing me and winning me back. Help me to see your grace and kindness, and respond by returning to you. Amen. –Andy Cimbala

Notes:

SHARING YOUR STORY - THE CALL OF THE PROPHETS

DAY 4   **RESTORATION.**   **JOEL 2:25**

"Then I will make up to you for the years that the swarming locust has eaten..." ESV

During the time of Joel the prophet, God's people had turned away from God. God tried several ways to get the attention of the people, even turning up the heat to the point of sending locusts that ate the crops, reminiscent of the plagues against Egypt during the Exodus. Still, God's people would not repent and return to God!

Joel steps onto the stage and speaks with God's authority, "Yet even now, return to me with all your heart, and with fasting, weeping and mourning; *rend your heart* and not your garments."[60] If they will return to God and repent, then God will pour out blessing! Not only will God stop the discipline and start the blessing, but God will make up to them all the difficulty that the discipline had brought. What a gracious God we have! God makes this crazy claim: even though it is our sin that has caused the locust plague, God will restore the years the locusts have eaten.

We do not serve a vindictive God, who delights in seeing us suffer. We serve a loving, kind, patient creator who knows what is best for us. When we return to God, God goes above and beyond in restoring us in a powerful way. God does this out of unconditional love for us, the very ones whom God created.

Reflection: Have you seen the consequences of your sin? Perhaps in broken relationships, or enslaving habits, or an embittered heart? Return to the Lord! Not only will God forgive you of your sins, but God even has the power to restore you.

Prayer: Merciful Lord, please forgive me for my many sins against you. I have such deaf ears. Thank you for calling me to return to you and being willing to restore me to a right relationship with you. Allow my heart to stir with joy and gratitude toward your mercy and grace. Amen. –Andy Cimbala

Notes:

---

60 Joel 2:12-13, ESV.

DAILY DEVOTIONALS - WEEK THREE

SHARING YOUR STORY - THE CALL OF THE PROPHETS

DAY 5   **SEEK THE LORD YOUR GOD WITH ALL YOUR HEART.** **DEUTERONOMY 4:29-31**

"But from there you will seek the LORD your God and you will find him, if you search after him with all your heart and with all your soul. When you are in tribulation, and all these things come upon you in the latter days, you will return to the LORD your God and obey his voice. For the LORD your God is a merciful God. He will not leave you or destroy you or forget the covenant with your fathers that he swore to them." NIV

Do we seek the Lord with all of our hearts? The time when I was farthest away from God was in my college days. Some of these occasions were when I was less than nice and other times when I was just not being faithful to God.

In particular, for me, it was my foul mouth. For a short period of time, mine was a sailor's mouth. One day I overheard another person speaking as I had for a few months. Suddenly, I realized that this one thing, even though seemingly so small, was not a reflection of the God who created me and not a reflection of who I wanted to be.

Sometimes we fail to pay attention to the small things that might lead us to stray from God, like the words that were coming out of my mouth which did not honor anyone, let alone the God of all creation. We look at the big things and we might think that we are in a good place, but God wants *all* of us. God wants us to turn our lives completely over to God. Little things whittle at our belief system, so much so that we can begin the erroneous thought of, "Well, that one little time will not matter." Maybe we begin to say, "This one little area of my life will be fine, even if it is not really what God wants."

The prophets are here to warn us of this false thinking. We are reminded by God to seek the Lord with all our heart and soul. God sent prophets to call the people and us back to a faithful God. In reality, we all need calling back to God. Belonging to God is a choice we make every day.

In sharing our God stories it is important that we also share that we do not have this following God thing down perfectly, but we are trying every day to follow God in a more authentic way.

Reflection: What small part of your life have you been trying to "keep from God?" Are you ready to turn it over and seek God with all your heart and soul in order to be a better reflection of your Lord and savior?

Prayer: God, you know I cannot do this on my own. Empower me by your Holy Spirit to turn every aspect of my life over to you, and to seek you with all of my heart and soul. Amen. -Rev. Dr. Sarah B. Dorrance

Notes:

SHARING YOUR STORY - THE CALL OF THE PROPHETS

DAY 6   **ASKING GOD TO SPEAK.**   **JEREMIAH 43:1-4**

"When Jeremiah finished speaking to all the people all these words of the LORD their God, with which the LORD their God had sent him to them, Azariah the son of Hoshaiah and Johanan the son of Kareah and all the insolent men said to Jeremiah, 'You are telling a lie. The LORD our God did not send you to say, 'Do not go to Egypt to live there,' but Baruch the son of Neriah has set you against us, to deliver us into the hand of the Chaldeans, that they may kill us or take us into exile in Babylon.'" ESV

Have you ever thought that life would be easier if God just *told* you what you should do next? Have you ever wanted God to directly speak into your situation and inform you which path to take? In the book of Jeremiah, chapters 42-43, God's people think the same thing. After the Babylonian army conquered Jerusalem, the remnant of survivors went to the prophet Jeremiah, whom they had ignored up until this point, and promised that if God told them what to do, they would obey this time. But do they follow through with their promise? After the Lord tells them distinctly to stay in the land and not to hide in Egypt, the people directly disobey. Even though God directly tells them all the blessing that God will pour upon them if they stay, they refuse. God's plan for their lives seems too scary, too hard, and too unclear.

While we may not have a modern day prophet like Jeremiah to tell us where God is directing us, we do have something better! We have the entire Old and New Testaments of the Bible and the recorded life and teaching of our savior Jesus Christ. God may not tell us exactly where we should go live or work as God did in Jeremiah 42-43, but God does tell us *what* we should be doing and the people with *whom* we should be engaging. In Matthew 28:19-20, Jesus tells us to, "Go and make disciples..." That may seem scary, hard, or unclear, but God promises blessing and success if we obey! God has directly *told* us what to do next. Will you choose to obey?

Reflection: Have you asked God to speak into your life? Is it possible that Scripture may already contain the answers that you are seeking? Do you, like me, "ask" God for direction when you already know what the answer should be? Are you following the command that God has spoken to you to make disciples? How can you make disciples in the places God has called you to be?

Prayer: God of wisdom and grace, so often I ask for you to speak, but in my fears and discomfort I forget that you have already spoken to me through your Word. Empower me to put my trust in you and to remember that you are with me forever, "until the end of the ages."[61] Amen. –Melissa Cimbala

Notes:

---

61 Matthew 28:21, ESV.

DAILY DEVOTIONALS - WEEK THREE

SHARING YOUR STORY - THE CALL OF THE PROPHETS

DAY 7   **STANDING AT THE CROSSROADS!**   **JEREMIAH 6:16**

"Stand at the crossroads and look; ask for the ancient paths, ask where the good way is, and walk in it, and you will find rest for your souls." NIV

Have you ever been on a path that had lost its directional sign and you had to determine the direction in which the route was headed? I like to hike. There have been multiple times, while out hiking in the mountains, that the path was not well marked or the sign had been broken. I was literally standing at a crossroads not certain which path was going to take me home and which path would take me deeper into the rough, wooded area of the mountain.

Sometimes we speak of a crossroad in life. This is a time when we have two very different paths that lead in opposite directions, and we have to determine which path to use. We often see those crossroads at intersections of life when we have major decisions to make. Which person should I marry? What should I do after high school? Should I quit this job and begin a different one that might be less lucrative, but would make me more content? There are so many questions and so many choices!

Sometimes, however, we stand at a crossroads and we do not recognize that it is a crossroad. Sometimes we are so busy doing the same old thing that we fail to acknowledge that if something does not change, the result from doing "the same old thing" is going to be disastrous.

This is where we are in many main-line denominations in America today. Christians are standing at a crossroads, and often we do not even recognize this as a crossroad. Sometimes we think, "If people would straighten up and be like us, this would be easy."

The reality is that we are standing at a crossroads of culture. Christians are the aliens. We are the folks who do not belong to this culture. How are we going to reach the nations for God if we cannot meet the culture where it is? What should we do differently? How will we reach through to our neighbors who have never heard the gospel message? What is the prophet calling *us* to do in our day and time?

One thing we can do at that crossroads is learn to tell our God stories. Another thing we can do is build relationships with those who are not inclined to attend a church where they can hear the gospel message. One thing we can do is learn to bless our neighbors. These are things we can do differently that will bring about change for good. We stand at a crossroads—pray to the LORD for direction and guidance.

Reflection: Do you feel like you are at a crossroads? In which direction do you intend to travel?

Prayer: God, empower me through your Holy Spirit to be able to reach across the divide of culture in order to be a part of your new creation on earth. Amen. –Rev. Dr. Sarah B. Dorrance

Notes:

SERMON OUTLINE - WEEK THREE

SHARING YOUR STORY - THE CALL OF THE PROPHETS

ISAIAH 55:6-12, JEREMIAH 6:16-19

1. Give a testimony of not following directions—mine was my daughter and hot stove.

    a. Told her not to touch, and what does she do?

    b. Intentional disobedience.

    c. That is part of our human nature, part of who we are.

        i. We saw that in the Garden of Eden, with Adam and Eve.

        ii. The nature of the human condition has a name—sin.

    d. Even children have this sinful nature, my four year old daughter disobeyed—sin.

2. The Israelites were no different; they disobeyed the God of covenant.

    a. We have been in a sermon series entitled, Sharing Your God Story.

    b. Two weeks ago we learned that God blessed Abraham for the purpose of Abraham sharing that blessing.

        i. Abraham was blessed with land.

        ii. He was blessed with offspring.

    c. Last week we learned that Abraham's offspring, called the Israelites and later called the Jews, were not to keep the blessing for themselves, but they were blessed to be a blessing to the nations.

    d. We learned that blessing has responsibility.

    e. We learned that God was faithful, even when they were unfaithful.

3. This week we see the unfaithfulness of the people come to full fruition.

    a. Even as God was faithful, the people were disobedient.

    b. We see this disobedience in this sentence from the book of Judges: "In those days there was no king in Israel. Everyone did what was right in his own eyes." (Judges 17:6)

        i. Friends, if that sentence doesn't scare us, it should. Look around us, in our culture, in our day.

        ii. Would you say those words apply to us?

4. There was an elaborate system of offering animal and grain sacrifices in the temple to cleanse one of sin.

    a. There was a very elaborate system of pilgrimage and cleansing and offering.

    b. It was works based. If you did this, in return you would be holy.

        i. Problem is, we know that we fail at works.

        ii. Even this elaborate system of sacrifice.

        iii. The Israelites found it too hard, too hard to be faithful in return.

        iv. In addition, they began to enjoy the fruits of prosperity.

SERMON OUTLINE - WEEK THREE

     1.   When we prosper, suddenly it is more difficult to share.

     2.   When we prosper, suddenly it is more difficult to say, "I am willing to share these blessings."

     3.   When we prosper, it is easier to forget about God and depend on self, rather than depend upon God. Old story attributed to Peter Marshall, chaplain to U.S. senate,

         a.   Man came and said, "When I was young and didn't make much money it was easy to tithe, it was easy to give God 10%, but now I make more and it is so much harder, it is a bigger amount. I am not sure I can part with that money."

         b.   Peter Marshall prayed with him, "Lord, reduce this man's salary so that he can tithe again."

         c.   Be careful what you pray for.

         d.   God has blessed us to share that blessing with others.

5.   In short, the people failed at sharing their blessings.

     a.   They failed at being witnesses for God. They failed at blessing the nations.

     b.   Even worse, they failed in remembering God, this faithful God who had brought them out of slavery, this faithful God to whom they promised their allegiance.

         i.   So God sent prophet after prophet to call them back into right relationship.

         ii.   Their works were not cutting it, because they were following the prescribed "works," yet still doing whatever they chose and not living according to God's ways. Remember those Ten Commandments? They were not ten suggestions. God really meant it when God gave those as the standards for living.

6.   Things went from bad to worse for the Israelites, prophets began foretelling of consequences for their sin. Disaster is going to fall upon you if you do not return to God.

     a.   God is going to use another nation, the Babylonians, to come, conquer, and destroy.

     b.   You can still prevent that if you turn back to God.

     c.   We see blessing, we have a responsibility to use the blessing well, and there are consequences.

     d.   Indeed, the Babylonian army did come: decimated Jerusalem, carried off the citizens as captives.

     e.   Known as the period of exile, where once again, they were strangers in a foreign land.

     f.   All is not lost. We hear Isaiah's words of promise, even when the Israelties are in exile. (Chapter 55: 6 - 12)

"Seek the LORD while he may be found; call on him while he is near. Let the wicked forsake their ways and the unrighteous their thoughts. Let them turn to the LORD, and he will have mercy on them, and to our God, for he will freely pardon.[8] "For my thoughts are not your thoughts, neither are your ways my ways," declares the LORD.[9] "As the heavens are higher than the earth, so are my ways higher than your ways and my thoughts than your thoughts. As the rain and the snow come down from heaven, and do not return to it without watering the earth and making it bud and flourish, so that it yields seed for the sower and bread for the eater, so is my word that goes out from my mouth: It will not return

to me empty, but will accomplish what I desire and achieve the purpose for which I sent it. You will go out in joy and be led forth in peace; the mountains and hills will burst into song before you, and all the trees of the field will clap their hands."

7. Think about that, God's word will not return empty.

   a. We know that when Jesus comes, which we will talk about next week, that Jesus is called the WORD that became flesh.

   b. Jesus, God in the flesh, God in human form, is the word.

   c. God's word, God's promise, God's faithfulness, will not return empty.

      i. What does that mean to you?

      ii. Can you think of a time or two when God was faithful to you?

      iii. Can you put those times into a story to be shared?

8. Here is the deal—

   a. In our day and time, we have the same pattern going on. People doing what they want to do according to their own eyes.

   b. We, as followers of Jesus, the one who changed the sacrificial system for us and became the sacrificial lamb for our sins, have the same responsibility as the Israelites—

   c. To be a blessing to those around us. To be a blessing to those in our neighborhoods and to point to God.

   d. United Methodists proclaim our covenant between us and God every time we have a new member or a baptism or bring young people into the Church through confirmation.

      i. The way United Methodists covenant together to be a blessing to the nations is through sharing our gifts of "prayers, presence, financial gifts, service and our witness." What does your denomination do?

      ii. This sermon series is about our witness, because we, as the larger church, have failed in this area.

      iii. We are not good witnesses, we are not good at sharing our stories.

         1. Maybe you disagree, but in response I would have to ask, how many times have you told a God story to someone you did not know this past week?

         2. If each of us told one God story each week, think of how this trend could be reversed!

9. So the prophet Jeremiah reminds us, we are standing at a crossroads:

   a. What will our response be?

   b. The people of Jeremiah's day chose to reject God and go a different way.

   "This is what the LORD says: 'Stand at the crossroads and look; ask for the ancient paths, ask where the good way is, and walk in it, and you will find rest for your souls.'" But you said, 'We will not walk in it.' I appointed watchmen over you and said 'Listen to the sound of the trumpet!' But you said, 'We will not listen.' Therefore hear, you nations; you who are witnesses, observe what will happen to them. Hear, you earth: I am bringing disaster on this people, the fruit of their schemes, because they have not listened to my words and have rejected my law." (Jeremiah 6:16-18, NIV)

SERMON OUTLINE - WEEK THREE

    c.   Our culture is beginning to do the same thing.

    d.   It is our job, it's our duty, it is part of our covenant, to tell our God stories.

10. Have you ever been at a crossroads?

    a.   I like to hike, more than once I have missed a sign and wondered which way the path would go.

    b.   If I chose the wrong path, it would lead to very different places.

    c.   Usually the wrong path would mean I was lost and would have a terrible time getting back to my starting point.

    d.   If you take the wrong path when hiking it could literally be the difference between life and death.

    e.   Friends, choose life.

         i.   Christianity today in America is also lost.

        ii.   The millennial population has now grown larger than the baby boomers, and yet the millennials are the most absent from church.

       iii.   They are the ones who have the largest percentage who check "none" when asked about religious affiliation.

       iv. What are we doing to share God with them?

11. Friends, for our main point, the time has come, we are standing at a crossroads, which direction will you choose?

    a.   Will you choose disobedience, like my daughter who burned her hand?

    b.   Or will you learn your God story or stories?

    c.   Will you learn how to share them?

         i.   This is God's mandate,

            1.   to be a blessing to the nations,

            2.   to point to God,

            3.   to be a reflection of who God is in the world,

        ii.   and we *have* to use words.

    d.   So, be bold, be courageous.

    e.   The Holy Spirit will empower you to tell your story and plant seeds for God's kingdom.

Amen.

LITURGY FOR WORSHIP - WEEK THREE

SHARING YOUR STORY - THE CALL OF THE PROPHETS

FIRST SCRIPTURE READING: ISAIAH 55:6-12

READING BEFORE THE SERMON: JEREMIAH 6:16-19; ISAIAH 42:10

CALL TO WORSHIP: (Based on Revelation 15:4)
Who shall not fear you, O LORD
And glorify your name?
For you alone are holy.
For all the nations shall come and worship before you,
For your judgments have been manifested.
Empower us, LORD, to be part of your greater design.
Your design that all the nations shall come to know you.
Give us courage to share our God stories so that the nations might come to know your saving grace.

PRAYER OF CONFESSION:
God of the Nations, We confess that we, too, like the Israelites, have strayed from your ways. You continually call us back into right relationship, yet we often put your voice on the back burner, preferring to attend to our own needs, wants, and desires. Empower us to hear the call of the prophets and to be faithful to you, even as you have been faithful to us. Lord, we desire to "rend our hearts unto you." Give us strength and courage, through the power of your Holy Spirit, to be fully yours. Amen.

POSSIBLE HYMNS:
57   O For a Thousand Tongues
110   A Mighty Fortress Is Our God
357   Just As I Am
395   Take Time to be Holy
397   I Need Thee Every Hour
400   Come Thou Fount of Every Blessing
428   For the Healing of the Nations
437   This Is My Song
2174   What Does the Lord Require
2108   O How He Loves You and Me
601   Thy Word
143   On Eagle's Wings

* *Two and three digit page numbers refer to the United Methodist Hymnal*
* *Four digit page numbers refer to The Faith We Sing Hymnal*

POSSIBLE PRAISE SONGS:
I Will Boast by Chris Tomlin
Blessed be Your Name by Matt Redman
Cornerstone by Hillsong United
The Stand by Hillsong United
I Will Follow by Chris Tomlin

Week Four
JESUS - Presence and Compassion

SMALL GROUP LEADER - WEEK FOUR

SHARING YOUR STORY - JESUS - PRESENCE AND COMPASSION

In the previous chapters we learned about God's blessing, the responsibility that comes with that blessing, and consequences. We learned that as inheritors of the blessing, we are always to point back to God, and be a blessing to the nations. We also learned that the people were not faithful to God, even as God was faithful to them. In the fullness of time, God sent his only Son, Jesus. The prophets had not been successful in calling the people back to right relationship with God. There was a period of silence when the Israelites did not hear from God, and then he came. He was not born of kings and queens, he was not born into royalty; rather God-in-the-flesh was born to peasants who were faithful to God. The Word became flesh and dwelt among us.[62] As he dwelt among us, he hung out with sinners like you and me. Jesus came to turn the known world's "systems" upside down. He was not part of the establishment, yet with his life, death, and resurrection he created a new world order; both in this life and the life to come.

Jesus came to die. He changed the sacrificial system of working for repentance. Instead of an elaborate system of temple sacrifice, he offered repentance for sins upon a cross where Jesus took all the sin and evil of the world upon himself, and he was victorious. Jesus was the one whose purpose was to offer himself on a cross, as the atonement for sin, so that we could all be in right relationship with God. This is the extreme offer of grace. You might be familiar with the verse from John 3 where Jesus tells a Pharisee named Nicodemus, "For God so loved the world that he gave his one and only Son, that whoever believes in him shall not perish but have eternal life."[63] Jesus offers grace, forgiveness, and mercy at the cross for all who believe in him.

But there is a follow up to that famous verse, which reminds us that Jesus came not to judge the world, but to save the world. Jesus then says, "For God did not send his Son into the world to condemn the world, but to save the world through him."[64] During the three-year ministry of Jesus, we see Jesus breaking bread with the outcast, the unloved, and the disenfranchised. We see Jesus showing us how to respond to the people who are in need of hope. As Jesus saves we see the beginning of the kingdom of God breaking out "on earth, as it is in heaven." This is the community formed by Jesus; this is the new creation; this is the reflection on earth as it is in heaven.[65] We are to continue the work begun by Jesus for building the new creation here on earth. This is how Jesus teaches us to be a blessing to the nations.

The Gospel of Matthew proclaims that Jesus "had compassion on them, because they were harassed and helpless, like sheep without a shepherd."[66] The ministry of Jesus unfolded in what theologian Bargil Pixner calls the "evangelical triangle,"[67] which is comprised of three villages: Capernaum, Bethsaida, and Chorazin.[68] These three villages were on the edge of the Sea of Galilee and are the sites for the bulk of Jesus' miracles. Pixner also lays out a convincing argument from the Gospel of Mark that Jesus himself went on three missionary trips from the Galilean area. Jesus went to the west coast to Tyre and Sidon, two cities which were not part of the Jewish communities. Jesus went north beyond Israelite territory to Caesarea Philippi, this is the place where Peter declared, "You are the Messiah."[69] In addition, Jesus went across the lake to the east to the region of the Gerasenes where he healed a man from a legion of

---

62 John 1:14, NIV.
63 John 3:16, NIV.
64 John 3:17, NIV.
65 Quote from *The Lord's Prayer*, Matthew 6:9-13, NIV.
66 Matthew 9:36, NIV.
67 Bargil Pixner, *With Jesus Through Galilee According to the Fifth Gospel*, (Rosh Pina, Israel, Corazin Publishing, 2005),p.87.
68 Luke 10:13, Matthew 11:21, NIV.
69 Mark 8:27-30, NIV.

demons.[70] It is important for us to understand that Jesus went beyond the chosen people of Israel. Jesus went beyond borders to draw all people into the fold. Jesus invited the Gentiles to be part of God's kingdom![71]

The ministry of Jesus was for all people. Matthew tells us that, "Jesus went throughout Galilee, teaching in their synagogues, proclaiming the good news of the kingdom, and healing every disease and sickness among the people. News about him spread all over *Syria*, and people brought to him all who were ill with various diseases, those suffering severe pain, the demon-possessed, those having seizures, and the paralyzed; and he healed them. Large crowds from *Galilee, the Decapolis*, Jerusalem, Judea and the *region across the Jordan* followed him."[72] These were people from all walks of life who were hungry for something more. They not only wanted to see the miracles performed by Jesus, but they wanted healing for themselves. They, too, wanted the hope, forgiveness, and mercy offered by the savior of the world. They were hungry not only for physical healing, but they were spiritually hungry. Jesus fed them in more ways than one.

Two stories, in particular, highlight the sharing of the good news with women who were not of the "chosen" people. This first story is that of a Greek woman, a Syrophoenician. [73] Why did she approach Jesus in the first place? She believed that Jesus could heal her daughter. Jesus even brings up the subject that he was first to go to the Israelites. Jesus does heal her daughter because of the woman's faith. Jesus had compassion for all people, and he did not discriminate in offering forgiveness, mercy, and healing.

A second story that highlights Jesus inviting all to participate in God's kingdom is when Jesus offered living water to the Samaritan woman at the well in the prime of day. The woman at the well was shunned by her community, and she was of a people group who did not get along with the Israelites. Yet Jesus offered her abundant grace.[74]

People from all walks of life came to be healed by Jesus. Jesus was not hiding in some castle, Jesus was not hard to get to, and Jesus was not hiding behind the closed doors of the synagogue. Jesus was walking around, in the streets, in fishing boats, walking to villages, always with the masses. The masses were hungry. They were hungry for spiritual food. Our spirit is a part of who we are, and it longs to be in right relationship with the one who created us. Jesus was offering new life!

The same is true in our day; our spirits are hungry. The spirits of those around us are hungry, but often we remain silent, hiding behind the four walls of our churches. Often we do not know where to begin in sharing our God stories or we think that a person we meet will not want to hear those stories. Perhaps we think that we do not have the correct words, but the Holy Spirit can provide us with the words we need. People we meet are spiritually hungry. They do not want to hear stories of judgment, but they do want to hear stories of compassion, hope, grace, and healing.

In our current day and culture, we share Jesus differently than at the turn of the 20th century. There were two routine models at the turn of that century for sharing Christ. In the first model, a charismatic speaker would present the gospel and call people to make a decision for Jesus. In the second model, Christians went knocking on doors to ask non-Christians leading questions in an effort to compel them

---

70 Mark 5.
71 It would be helpful for students to look closely at these areas on a map.
72 Matthew 4:23-25, NIV.
73 Mark 7:24-30, NIV.
74 John 4.

to receive Jesus. Those forms of evangelism or sharing the gospel message might have worked then, but they have become less effective in our current culture. In fact, many of our modern day Christians shun these methodologies, and in turn, the word "evangelism" has received a bad name.

Theologian Mark Driscoll argues for a new way of sharing Christ which he calls "Reformation Participation Evangelism."[75] This style of sharing Jesus relies on the fact that many young people in our culture want to belong before they believe. So, the job of the Christian today is to build relationships. We invite folks in order to form community, or maybe we invite them to a small group. Then, they in turn, learn the full message of the gospel. Another way to build relationships through the church is through "on ramps." These are events, either missional in nature or community-oriented, that are designed to build relationships for the purpose of sharing the gospel. Small community groups that are "open" groups are a key way in which to build relationships with those outside our spheres of influence. In short, the way people used to come to know Christ was that they would first believe through a preacher, a revival, or a gospel tract, and then they would want to belong to a community of believers. Now, in our culture, it is very different. Now people want to belong. They long to belong, and, it is in the midst of that belonging that they are introduced to the person of Jesus Christ.

At the end of the earthly ministry of Jesus, after he had been crucified, buried, and raised from the dead, the resurrected Christ gives us a commission. This commission is for all believers, not just a few, not just some. Each gospel writer tells us this commission in a different way, but they each give us the commission. We are to be a sent people. John tells us, "Jesus said, 'Peace be with you! As the Father has sent me, I am sending you.'"[76] Matthew gives us the Great Commission. "Then the eleven disciples went to Galilee, to the mountain where Jesus had told them to go. When they saw him, they worshiped him; but some doubted. Then Jesus came to them and said, 'All authority in heaven and on earth has been given to me. Therefore go and make disciples of all nations, baptizing them in the name of the Father and of the Son and of the Holy Spirit, and teaching them to obey everything I have commanded you. And surely I am with you always, to the very end of the age.'"[77] In the book of Acts we are told exactly where we are to share our God stories and we are told by what power we can share them. "But you will receive power when the *Holy Spirit* comes on you; and you will *be my witnesses in Jerusalem, and in all Judea, and Samaria, and to the ends of the earth.*"[78]

God sent Jesus, and in return we are to be a sent people, empowered by the Holy Spirit. We are to be missionaries where we are in our corners of the earth, and beyond, for a broken world. God in the flesh helps draw out the God stories of all people. Here is the reality: God gives us God stories to tell so that others might come into a saving relationship with Jesus Christ. We each have God stories so that we can do our part in ushering in God's kingdom here on earth, so that we can do our part in sharing the good news of Jesus—that we are forgiven and free. This gift of grace is not for us to hoard and keep for ourselves. This is the historical intersection of God's story and your story. Just like the blessing given to Abraham and his descendants, these God stories are to be shared with our neighbors, the cities, and the nations. Are you willing to be a blessing and share your story? Jesus gives us the power of the Holy Spirit so that we can be courageous, so that we can be given the right words, so that we can offer life anew and hope, to those who are broken. What will you choose to do?

---

75 Mark Driscoll, *The Radical Reformission: Reach Out Without Selling Out.* (Grand Rapids, MI, Zondervan Press, 2004), p. 68.
76 John 20:21, NIV.
77 Matthew 28:16-20, NIV.
78 Acts 1:8, NIV.

SMALL GROUP LEADER DISCUSSION - WEEK FOUR

1. Unpack the verse from John 3:17. How have modern day Christians been judgmental in recent years?

    a. How has judging others been reflected in our churches?

    b. Are our churches safe places for open discussion that is real and relevant to people's lives?

    c. How have we reflected judgmentalism back onto Jesus?

2. As the Father has sent me, so I send you.

    a. What does that statement mean to you?

    b. How are we a sent people?

3. What do you think of the statement that we used to believe and then belong, now we belong to a faith community and then we come to believe?

4. Do you know Jesus? Have you accepted Jesus as your Lord and Savior? If you have not received Jesus as your Lord and Savior, this would be a good time to repent and turn your life over to Christ.

    a. Think about it, pray about it. The prayer below could be a model.

    b. Dear Jesus, I want to belong to you. Forgive me for my selfish ways and my sins. Thank you for dying on a cross to offer me forgiveness. I offer my life both past and present to you. Come and be Lord of my life, and thank you for accepting me as I am. Empower me, through the Holy Spirit, to grow more and more like you. Amen.

5. Read together the story of the Greek woman from Syrophoenicia. Mark 7:24.

    a. Do the words of Jesus seem harsh to you?

    b. What do you think is behind this exchange of words?

6. Read John 4:1-42.

    a. What strikes you as odd about this story?

    b. What did the disciples think when they heard Jesus talking to a woman from Samaria?

7. Compare the four versions of the Great Commission in each of the gospels. What do you find different and what seems to be the same? Matthew 28:16-20; Mark 16:14-20; Luke 24:44-49; and John 20:19-23.

DAILY DEVOTIONALS - WEEK FOUR

SHARING YOUR STORY - JESUS - PRESENCE AND COMPASSION

DAY 1   **THE SYROPHOENICIAN WOMAN'S FAITH.**   **MARK 7:24-30**

"From there he set out and went away to the region of Tyre. He entered a house and did not want anyone to know he was there. Yet he could not escape notice, but a woman whose little daughter had an unclean spirit immediately heard about him, and she came and bowed down at his feet. Now the woman was a Gentile, of Syrophoenician origin. She begged him to cast the demon out of her daughter. He said to her, 'Let the children be fed first, for it is not fair to take the children's food and throw it to the dogs.' But she answered him, 'Sir, even the dogs under the table eat the children's crumbs.' Then he said to her, 'For saying that, you may go—the demon has left your daughter.' So she went home, found the child lying on the bed, and the demon gone." NRSV

When most of us hear a prayer request for healing, our minds automatically go to physical healing such as healing of cancer, surgery, broken bones, and so on. We tend to overlook healings that are needed in other areas of people's journeys. The Syrophoenician woman's daughter had a demon. The gospel writers tell us that Jesus had the ability to cast out demons, and that he did so frequently. This mother's persistence showed her faith and Jesus healed her daughter because of the mother's determined faith.

How strong is your faith? When you do not perceive your prayers being answered in what you consider to be a timely manner, does your faith begin to dwindle or does it stay strong in knowing and believing that God will answer and that God's answer will be for God's glory?

The way our prayers are answered is God's story. Our response to God's answers is our story, and the two create the story of love and grace between a parent and a child.

Reflection: What is your response when God seemingly does not answer your prayers? What is your response when the answer is positive and a great miracle has occurred? Do you share those stories with others?

Prayer: Loving God, forgive me for doubting your power and presence in my time of need. Help me realize that I may not understand your answers to my prayers, but to face those answers with courage and the knowledge of your love for me. Amen. –Pastor Lynn Wilson

Notes:

DAILY DEVOTIONALS - WEEK FOUR

SHARING YOUR STORY - JESUS - PRESENCE AND COMPASSION

DAY 2   **LET THE REDEEMED TELL THEIR STORY!**   **PSALM 107:1-3**

"Give thanks to the LORD, for he is good; his love endures forever. Let the redeemed of the LORD tell their story—those he redeemed from the hand of the foe, those he gathered from the lands, from east and west, from north and south." NIV

My friend Angel gave permission to use her story. She says, "God is so awesome. Yep. Thirteen years ago I had brain surgery for a pretty serious looking brain tumor. Following that surgery in April of 2002, we were told the tumor was successfully excised. Just two short days later, I was released from the hospital and found out a week later that though it was considered a grade 2 (out of 4) tumor, pre-surgical MRI scans showed it was a more aggressive tumor. I then went through treatments of chemo and radiation. After almost two full years of treatment, and over 50 follow-up MRI scans to check for recurrence, and many, many, prayers later, I am still tumor free! God is good! I pray that how I live my life, now, shows God how amazingly grateful I am for this blessing."

We never know from day to day what will happen in our lives that will become a part of our greater story. My friend Angel did not dream that she would have a brain tumor diagnosis, and go through brain surgery, radiation, and chemo. When I asked her about using her story in this devotion she did not hesitate, but she wanted to make sure that it is understood that her story should be used and told to bring God praise. Angel not only gives God praise and glory for her healing, but also for bringing her beloved husband Jim safely home through multiple deployments during his military career.

Reflection: Do you let others know what a wonderful God you serve and how you have been healed or touched by God? Sometimes we think that those parts of our story aren't important because they are specific to our lives. Who wants to hear about my life? Sometimes we might think that we are boring people with our stories, however, if we are being faithful, observant, and most importantly listening to God, we will find ourselves at the right time, right place, and right audience to tell the part of our healing story that God wants to be known, and all the glory will go to God.

Prayer: Give me the wisdom to know what part of and when to humbly share *our* story, Lord. Give me the strength and courage to tell others that without your healing and strength, I would not even have a story. Amen. –Pastor Lynn Wilson

Notes:

DAILY DEVOTIONALS - WEEK FOUR

SHARING YOUR STORY - JESUS - PRESENCE AND COMPASSION

DAY 3   **PEACE IN THE PROMISES OF JESUS.**   **JOHN 16:33**

"I have said this to you, so that in me you may have peace. In the world you face persecution. But take courage; I have conquered the world!" NRSV

There are times when we do not go to God with our pain or hurt because we do not think that our hurt or infirmity is important enough to bring before our creator. Sometimes we feel that if our illness is not the size of a mountain then God will not have time for it. We unwisely choose to try to handle the small things on our own, which often leads the small things to grow into large things. Maybe we feel as though the pain or hurt we are having is deserved because we have either failed those we love, or we feel we have failed ourselves, or we might even feel we have failed God. My friends, I am so thankful that God's love for me is not based on what I deserve but on God's freely given grace. We do not always understand that there is nothing too small or too big to take to our Lord in prayer. Please know that God is aware of our issue/s before we speak it, regardless of magnitude. God's desire for us is that we find our peace in Jesus' promises to us, as seen in today's Scripture. The only way we will truly find rest or peace is when we look toward Jesus as the healer. We will find pain and hurt in this world, but we need to always remember that our Lord conquered the world, and the victory of Jesus is the only lasting cure.

Reflection: Where do you need peace today? What small or big thing needs to be brought before our Lord today?

Prayer: Forgive me, Jesus, for not trusting you with everything in my life regardless of size. Thank you for being the cure, and bring me the peace that only you can offer. Amen. –Pastor Lynn Wilson

Notes:

DAILY DEVOTIONALS - WEEK FOUR

SHARING YOUR STORY - JESUS - PRESENCE AND COMPASSION

DAY 4   **MORE THAN CONQUERORS.**   **ROMANS 8:37-39**

"Yet in all these things we are more than conquerors through Jesus who loved us. For I am persuaded that neither death nor life, nor angels nor principalities nor powers, nor things present nor things to come, nor height nor depth, nor any other created thing, shall be able to separate us from the love of God which is in Christ Jesus our Lord." Life Application Bible

The Life Application Bible reminds us that, "These verses contain one of the most comforting promises in all Scripture. Believers have always had to face hardships in many forms: persecution, illness, imprisonment, even death. These could cause them to fear that they have been abandoned by Christ. But Paul exclaims that it is impossible to be separated from Christ. Christ's death for us is proof of unconquerable love. Nothing can stop Christ's constant presence with us. God tells us how great God's love is so that we will feel totally secure in God. If we believe these overwhelming assurances, we will not be afraid."[79]

Fear causes us to mistrust God's love for us, it makes us ill. Paul reminds us that we can let go of fear and we can face our trials head on knowing that God is with us. As Christians, our stories do not have to stand on their own. Other stories of suffering join ours. Jesus' story of the ultimate suffering is there as well. We are not alone. We have each other, and more importantly we have the love of God and God's story to help us through. There is a plaque that hangs on my office door that reads, "Life isn't about waiting for the storm to pass...It's about learning to dance in the rain." As long as we allow God to lead the dance we will keep in step and end gracefully in the arms of Jesus.

Reflection: What fears do you need to let go of today? Close your eyes, and imagine the presence of Jesus with you. Ask Jesus to take away your fears and to be a constant abiding presence in your life.

Prayer: Blessed Jesus, help me to release the fear that sometimes grips me causing me to lose timing and doubt your healing power and blessed grace. Create in me the strength to splash through the puddles of life until we meet in your kingdom. Amen. –Pastor Lynn Wilson

Notes:

---

79 Life Application Bible, (Tyndale Press), 1993, p. 2071.

DAILY DEVOTIONALS - WEEK FOUR

SHARING YOUR STORY - JESUS - PRESENCE AND COMPASSION

DAY 5   **SPIRITUAL HEALTH.**   **MATTHEW 9:1-2**

"Jesus stepped into a boat, crossed over and came to his own town. Some men brought to him a paralyzed man, lying on a mat. When Jesus saw their faith, he said to the man, 'Take heart, son; your sins are forgiven." NIV

When the paralyzed man was brought to Jesus, the first thing Jesus said to him was "Your sins are forgiven." Jesus' first concern was with the man's spiritual health. When we allow our spiritual health to weaken, we lose our strength to fight what this world throws at us. Our ability to endure physical, emotional, or relational issues weakens and we end up digging ourselves into an early grave. For a moment pretend that your spiritual life can be gauged by weights, one pound through 66 pounds. (One pound=one book of the Bible or one chapter of the story). Each pound represents the amount of time spent in building your spiritual health. As spiritual weight lifters if we do not lift weights regularly then we become weak and do not have the strength to conquer the enemy. Through the power of the Holy Spirit, and with regular spiritual exercise, we become stronger and eventually we will lift those 66 pounds with less effort while being able to provide more impact. We become less intimidated with worldly factors because we have gained the confidence and spiritual strength required to stand up to the worldly woes in a Christian manner.

Reflection: The Bible is our set of exercise weights to strengthen our spiritual body. Do you exercise your ailing spiritual body regularly? Are you getting stronger so you can be used by God?

Prayer: Blessed Savior, forgive me for not being faithful to my spiritual health. Grant me the desire to be more attentive to the strength that can only be increased through you. Amen. –Pastor Lynn Wilson

Notes:

DAILY DEVOTIONALS - WEEK FOUR

SHARING YOUR STORY - JESUS - PRESENCE AND COMPASSION

DAY 6   **THE HANDS OF JESUS.**   **LUKE 7:14-15**

"Then he went up and touched the bier they were carrying him on, and the bearers stood still. He said, 'Young man, I say to you, get up!' The dead man sat up and began to talk, and Jesus gave him back to his mother." NIV

Jesus restores life to a woman's dead son. Jesus touched the bier, which is a stand on which a casket containing a corpse is placed to be carried to the grave. Jesus restored life! Have you ever thought about what the healing, restorative hands of Jesus looked like? Have you ever thought about what Jesus' physical touch would have felt like? My imagination sees rough, worn, calloused, tanned, hands that have been subjected to hard days of physical labor as a carpenter. After the crucifixion, those same hands would have holes in them where spikes were driven to hold Jesus' body on the cross. Those hands reach out to comfort us in our times of need and sorrow. Those same hands are the hands that work through us as we share the story of Jesus. Those same hands are the ones that clasp ours as we provide healing touches to others in their time of need, bringing Jesus' story, our story, and the one to whom we are sharing the story together. Rough, worn, and torn hands that provide a love far greater than we can imagine.

Reflection: Many times just the touch of a hand is all of the healing necessary to change a life. Do you provide this kind of healing? No, but the one who does can work through your touch, through the power of the Holy Spirit, to heal and make new. Are you willing to give your hands over to Jesus?

Prayer: Jesus, open my eyes and show me how and where you can use my hands. Let them be an instrument of your healing power. Amen. –Pastor Lynn Wilson

Notes:

DAILY DEVOTIONALS - WEEK FOUR

SHARING YOUR STORY - JESUS - PRESENCE AND COMPASSION

DAY 7   **UNITED IN JESUS!**   **HEBREWS 13:15-16**

"Through Jesus, therefore, let us continually offer to God a sacrifice of praise—the fruit of lips that openly profess his name. And do not forget to do good and to share with others, for with such sacrifices God is pleased." NIV

Someday all who profess the name of Jesus as their Lord and Savior will be set free from all earthly sufferings. One of my favorite old hymns is "There Will be Peace in the Valley." The chorus is as follows:

> There will be peace in the valley for me, some day
> There will be peace in the valley for me, oh Lord I pray
> There'll be no sadness, no sorrow
> No trouble, trouble I see
> There will be peace in the valley for me, for me.

We will all be healed from whatever ails us. God's stories and our stories will join in an unending hymn of praise. Until that time, my prayer is that we are all willing to be disciples of Jesus Christ, sharing our stories of Jesus' healing power for the glory of God.

Reflection: Will you allow God to use you? Will you be the healing hands of Jesus to your family, friends, and the stranger on the street?

Prayer: Almighty and gracious God, I thank you for your story and the story you have given me. I pray that I will see my weaknesses and allow you to take them away and strengthen my faith. Help me to keep my body physically strong and my mind and soul spiritually strong. Take away the fears that I may have in serving you. Help me, Lord, be open to you as you use my hands, and God stories, to help others realize your love for them. In your name, blessed Jesus, I pray. Amen. –Pastor Lynn Wilson

Notes:

SERMON OUTLINE - WEEK FOUR

SHARING YOUR STORY - JESUS - PRESENCE AND COMPASSION

MATTHEW 9:35-38 AND MARK 7: 24-30

1. Testimony about Pastor Rodney Hudson: (I used the Baltimore riots as a testimony to God's action and presence. The preacher should use a relevant story that reflects what is happening at the time.)

   a. Rodney was called out by God to serve the UMC church—

   b. He serves Ames UMC, right down in Sandtown—where the riots have taken place.

   c. He is serving the folks at Sandtown

   d. Before this past week's events ever happened, Rodney was in the streets sharing the good news about Jesus.

      i. One of the kids on the corner that Rodney met was Freddie Gray.

      ii. Pastor Rodney is a pastor who continues to help these kids know there is more to life than hanging on the street, there is more, there is Jesus.

      iii. "I pause to reflect on the early days of meeting Freddie Gray. I met him in July 2008 on the corner of Baker and Carey Street. Freddie along with the other young boys were working their shift on the corner across the street from Ames Memorial Church. For an entire year, Ames Church conducted outside revivals, prayer meetings, food distributions, and daily conversations with the young boys who reluctantly moved their operations to another area of the community. Although there were many days that Freddie and the rest of the young men became frustrated with our outreach ministry, they respected the church and our leaders enough to not resort to violence. That respect speaks to the long history and outreach of the Ames Memorial Church's influence in the Sandtown community."

2. This story is important in light of our sermon series, entitled Sharing Your God Story.

   a. The sermon series we have been in reminds us that we all have a story that needs to be shared.

   b. We have learned that from the beginning, God created us to be in relationship with God and with one another.

   c. From the beginning God promised blessing, and there was a responsibility with that blessing.

   d. Last week we saw that the prophets were continually calling the Israelites back to right relationship with God, and they warned of consequences. Those consequences became a reality and the people found themselves, once again, as strangers in a foreign land.

   e. In our sermon today, we see that, in the fullness of time, God became flesh, to change this system of sacrifice, and to usher in a new era.

      i. This is something new, through Jesus.

      ii. Jesus came to usher in a new age, a new age of offering the kingdom of God, a new age of being in right relationship with God and each other.

      iii. A new age of being a sent people.

      iv. A new age of offering compassion and presence.

3. Jesus began this three year ministry telling folks that the kingdom of God was near.

SERMON OUTLINE - WEEK FOUR

    a.   Immediately after Jesus was baptized by John the Baptist and after the wilderness experience and temptation of Jesus, these are the words we hear from Matthew 4:

        i.   "Jesus went throughout Galilee, teaching in their synagogues, proclaiming the good news of the kingdom, and healing every disease and sickness among the people. News about him spread all over Syria, and people brought to him all who were ill with various diseases, those suffering severe pain, the demon-possessed, those having seizures, and the paralyzed; and he healed them. Large crowds from Galilee, the Decapolis, Jerusalem, Judea and the region across the Jordan followed him."

        ii.   Note, these are people coming from all areas to be healed by Jesus. These are people who are from beyond the Israelites' borders.

        iii.   (Show a map to see where "the Israelites" were found.) (Show a map of the area around the Sea of Galilee.)

4.   We continually see Jesus having compassion on all people, and training them to become the spark that ushers in the kingdom of God. Jesus trains them to be harvesters of souls. Jesus trains them to have compassion on the people. Later, in Matthew 9: 35 - 38, we hear these words:

    a.   "Jesus went through all the towns and villages, teaching in their synagogues, proclaiming the good news of the kingdom and healing every disease and sickness. When he saw the crowds, he had compassion on them, because they were harassed and helpless, like sheep without a shepherd. Then he said to his disciples, 'The harvest is plentiful but the workers are few. Ask the Lord of the harvest, therefore, to send out workers into his harvest field.'"

    b.   He had compassion on them, like sheep without a shepherd.

    c.   What are our thoughts when we see the destruction by Baltimore riots?

    d.   We grieve, we wonder, but do we have compassion?

        i.   Do we have compassion for systems that are broken and need fixing?

        ii.   Compassion for both "sides", police, people—caught in a culture that is a vicious cycle.

        iii.   Do we have compassion for people who are caught up in an economic disparity that seems to have no end?

            1.   I am not into politics, but I am into seeing people through the eyes of Jesus.

            2.   I am a proponent of looking deep into the eyes of someone and asking, "How can I serve you?"

            3.   People in our cities need something to change, people who are keeping law and order need a change. We are broken.

5.   Jesus understood the brokenness of the world. Jesus came to usher in a new age. Jesus himself went on mission trips beyond the Sea of Galilee to engage with the people. There are some who believe that Jesus went on three mission trips. You can learn more about those trips in the small group studies, but one such trip was when Jesus went to Tyre and Sidon.

"Jesus left that place and went to the vicinity of Tyre. He entered a house and did not want anyone to know it; yet he could not keep his presence secret. In fact, as soon as she heard about him, a woman whose little daughter was possessed by an impure spirit came and fell at his feet. The woman was a Greek, a Syrophoenician by birth. She begged Jesus to drive the demon out of her daughter. 'First let the children eat all they want,' he told her, 'for it is not right to take the children's bread and toss it to the dogs.' 'Lord,' she replied, 'even the dogs under the table eat the children's crumbs.' Then he told her, 'For such a reply, you may go; the demon has left your daughter.' She went home and found her child lying on the bed, and the demon gone."(Mark 7:27).

    a.   Friends, this woman was clearly not a woman of the "chosen" people, but she had faith, she believed that Jesus could do something.

    b.   Moms and dads, we are in despair if our kids are hurting, are we not?

    c.   We would go to any length to empower our kids, to help our kids live.

    d.   Note that Jesus did three things:

        i.   He was present.

        ii.   He had compassion.

        iii.   And he listened to her story...

            1.   He sees the depth of her faith.

            2.   He sees the depth of her faith that says something here can be different.

            3.   He sees the depth of her faith that says, I know YOU, Jesus, can change this situation.

6.   Friends, over these past few weeks we have been speaking about how to share our stories.

    a.   We have asked the question, "What would it look like if I shared a God story?"

    b.   In addition, we have been reminded that we first have to build relationships and trust in order to share those God stories.

        i.   What would it look like if we took these three things that Jesus did, and applied them to people we meet?

        ii.   We have to be present...fully present.

        iii.   We need a changed heart that allows for compassion.

        iv.   We need to be able to listen to others, in order to hear their stories, and then, at the right time, we are invited to tell our own story of Jesus.

            1.   Because here is the deal, we don't earn the right to tell our stories without first listening to a story from someone else.

            2.   When you first listen to another's story, you then earn the right to tell your own story.

7.   Think of how things can be different in Baltimore if we practice those three things:

    a.   Presence, compassion, and listening...

    b.   We have United Methodists doing that right now with the people on the streets.

    c.   Pastor Rodney is on the front lines. This is what else he says about the area he is serving

    d.   "Although Sandtown is in close proximity to the famed Pennsylvania Avenue where personalities like Frederick Douglass, Billie Holiday, and Thurgood Marshall had trodden down its streets once paved with proverbial gold; today, however, these same streets are littered with potholes accessorized with beer cans, spent condoms, used needles, and trash. Sadly, nearly 50% of Sandtown's residents live below the poverty level, 50% unemployment rate, 77% high school dropout rate, and the community has been ranked among neighborhoods with the highest crime rates in the State of Maryland. Consequently, the socioeconomic disparities coupled with the lack of adequate space to conduct ministry have made Sandtown unattractive to mainline denominational faith communities and faith leaders some of whom have been lured away by the sensual hemlines of middle class prosperity. With declining memberships, delayed building repairs, and low economic resources, it is no surprise that some churches have no choice but to relocate in order to survive. The end result has resulted in limited missional outreach, limited pastoral presence in the community, and more church closures by mainline denominations."

    e. We can lift him and the church he serves, Ames Memorial, up in prayer every day, along with our other churches in Baltimore and Chicago and Detroit and...

    f. We can make health kits, and we can make a positive impact financially.

    g. Another way we can respond is to listen, build a connection with someone who is different from you.

    h. And then you will be invited to share your story.

    i. That, my friends, is how we build relationships that allow us to enter into the conversation of sharing Jesus, and then, of making disciples.

8. Jesus came to die, so that we might live.

    a. Jesus came to die so that we might see the power of resurrection in this current life and life beyond.

    b. Jesus came to offer new life, in the here and now, and beyond.

9. How do we offer that new life now?

    a. By understanding that Jesus now sends us on that mission. Jesus says, "as the father has sent me, so I send you."

    b. **Jesus commissions us to go make disciples.**

    c. **We can only be a sent people if we understand that we are to share our stories.**

    d. We can only be a sent people if we understand that we have to go out and be the missional church, the attractional model no longer works...we are a SENT people.

        i. Attractional is the one who sits and waits for people to arrive.

        ii. Missional is the one who goes out into the community and has "on ramps" during which people can build relationships.

            1. What are "on ramps?"

            2. They are opportunities to get involved with the body of Christ outside of worship.

            3. Sometimes an "on ramp" might be a community service project.

            4. Sometimes an "on ramp" might be a small group.

        iii. That is what sent means, being missional in nature. What are we as the body of Christ doing?

    e. We can only be a sent people if we understand that we are all part of God's missionary team.

10. Pastor Rodney understands that... Every day, out in the streets, sharing the good news.

    a. Every day, out in the streets saying, "something can change, and we can be a part of it."

    b.   Every day out there saying "Jesus offers us something more, life anew."

11. We close today with a poem written by my friend, fellow Elder and the United Methodist Church District Superintendent at Baltimore.

    a.   I have been in many prayer conference calls with her at ten p.m.

    b.   This is her poem, reminding us who Jesus calls us to be in sharing our stories

I AM MISSION
(by Rev. Dr. Wanda Bynum Duckett)

COMING FROM A HIP PLACE INTO THIS PLACE
INTO YOUR SPACE, ON A MISSION CALLED LIFE

CALLED TO GIVE UP MINE, SO THAT IN TIME
YOU WOULD UNDERSTAND THAT I COME TO MAKE READY

SO ROCK STEADY...THAT'S WHAT I FEEL, THAT'S WHAT I AM
I'M A ROCK...OF ALL, IN ALL, TO ALL AGES...READ THE PAGES

EAT THE BREAD THAT I AM, THE LIFE THAT I AM
THE TRUTH THAT I AM. I AM. I AM MISSION.

LIGHT OF THE WORLD I AM. I SHINE FOR I AM.
AND YOU SHINE TOO...SO TO YOU BE TRUE!
BUT NEVER FORGET THAT I AM. I AM MISSION.

I AM THE DOOR WHEN EVERYTHING IS ON LOCK.
I AM THE SHEPHERD LOOKING OUT FOR MY FLOCK.
I AM THE RESURRECTION SO THAT YOU TOO CAN RISE.
MY TRUTH SHAMES LIES. DARK CLOUDS DESPISE
BUT NEVERTHELESS I AM. I AM MISSION.

MAKE WAY FOR I AM...
THAT WAY, THE ONE WAY, THE ONLY WAY TRUTH AND LIFE ETERNAL, EVERLASTING
THOUGH GUN SHOTS ARE BLASTING,
THOUGH SOME FOLKS ARE FASTING
WHILE OTHERS HAVE PLENTY TO EAT.
I AM...I AM MISSION.
IN DROUGHT, I AM WATER, THROUGH CHAOS, I AM ORDER
TO THE NATIONS I AM PEACE. I AM "MOS DEF" TO THE LEAST

BECAUSE I COME FROM A HIP PLACE
INTO YOUR SPACE...ON A MISSION
THEY WERE JUST FISHIN...BUT I DON'T JUST COME, I SEND.
SO GO...FEED...TEACH...FREE...BUILD...LOVE...FOR...ME
THROUGH ME ALL THINGS ARE POSSIBLE!
FOR I AM. I AM MISSION.

LITURGY FOR WORSHIP - WEEK FOUR

SHARING YOUR STORY - JESUS: PRESENCE AND COMPASSION

FIRST SCRIPTURE READING: GALATIANS 3:7-9

READING BEFORE THE SERMON: GENESIS 12:1-5A

CALL TO WORSHIP:
(Based on Matthew 9:35-38)

Jesus, enter into our sanctuary.
Teach us, too, Lord, teach us too!
Sometimes we feel broken and lost in this world,
Sometimes, we, too, feel like sheep without a shepherd.
We long to be in your presence,
We long to hear your voice.
Have compassion on us,
So that we might know your presence and share the good news of the kingdom of God with others.
Empower us to be workers to harvest souls for you.

PRAYER OF CONFESSION:
Lord of the Harvest, we confess that all too often we are occupied with our own worries and concerns and we forget your bigger picture, your greater plan. Lord, guide our thoughts and minds towards kingdom building, understanding you have a great design for each of us. Allow us to see others as you see them, each part of your beloved creation. Raise us up, Lord, to glean a harvest of souls for the kingdom of God. Empower us by your Holy Spirit to fulfill your Great Commission of making disciples of the nations. Amen.

POSSIBLE HYMNS:
57   O For a Thousand Tongues to Sing
585   This Little Light of Mine
584   Lord, You Give the Great Commission (You could do this to the tune of 581)
428   For the Healing of the Nations
431   Let There Be Peace on Earth
504   Old Rugged Cross
593   Here I Am Lord

* Two and three digit page numbers refer to the United Methodist Hymnal

POSSIBLE PRAISE SONGS:
Jesus at the Center by Israel Houghton
Jesus Messiah by Chris Tomlin
Shine, Jesus, Shine
Go, by Hillsong United
All Because of Jesus
Amazing Grace (My Chains are Gone)
Grace so Glorious by Elevation Worship
White Flag

Week Five
The Church - Bold and Bodacious

SMALL GROUP LEADER - WEEK FIVE

SHARING YOUR STORY - THE CHURCH - BOLD AND BODACIOUS

"As the Father is sending me, I am sending you!"[80] Those are Jesus' words to his disciples. All those who profess Jesus as Lord and Savior eventually learn that there is responsibility with the blessing of being called God's people. God's story is redefined by the resurrected Christ to remind each of us that our obligation is to understand that we are a sent people. With blessing comes responsibility. That responsibility is to be a witness for the one who sends us; that responsibility is to make disciples for Jesus Christ; that responsibility is to bless others even as we have been blessed; that responsibility is to share our God stories.

We cannot move out of our comfort zones as an act of our own will when sharing our God stories. However, there is more Good News, Jesus promises that he will not leave us as orphans.[81] The third person of the trinity, the Holy Spirit, came to fall upon believers in order to empower them—in order to empower us—to act beyond our human scope of abilities.

The Holy Spirit is perhaps the most misunderstood person of the Trinitarian God. The Spirit is a "power," it "leads," it "testifies," it "makes known," it "drives Jesus to the wilderness," it "speaks," it is the "advocate" and the "comforter," to name but a few.[82] It is referred to as both the "Spirit of Christ" in 1 Peter 1:11 and the "Spirit of God" in 1 Peter 4:14 and 1 John 4:2-3. The full biblical witness is required to gain any understanding of the Doctrine of the Holy Spirit. One thing for sure, the Holy Spirit gives us courage to tell our God stories, and, when we cannot find the words, the Holy Spirit can empower us with the right words and the right part of our stories that will touch the lives of others.

There is freedom in new life with the Holy Spirit. The Spirit frees us to have a new mind in Christ. It is through this freedom that we are able to love God and to love others in right relationship. Migliore says, "The Spirit frees believers for a pattern of life that reflects the pattern of God's self-giving love in Jesus Christ."[83] It is by the power of the Holy Spirit that we are able to share our God stories in new and powerful ways.

While the Holy Spirit was active from the beginning of time, in Acts chapter 2 we see the Spirit of God fall on believers in a powerful new way. Peter, who was among the disciples who fell asleep when Jesus was in fervent prayer; who was the disciple who denied Jesus; who was the one nowhere to be seen during the crucifixion of Jesus; is empowered in new ways by the Holy Spirit. Suddenly we see Peter, now bold and bodacious, speaking on behalf of God.[84] This man who had denied Jesus is now becoming, as Jesus predicted, the rock upon which the church will be built. Do not miss the words that Jesus promises, "And I tell you that you are Peter, and on this rock I will build my church, and the gates of Hades will not overcome it."[85] This man Peter is preaching in languages he did not learn, this man is performing miracles in ways not previously available to him, and this man is not afraid of authoritative figures who might crucify him as well.

As believers, we acknowledge the power and authority of the Holy Spirit in our daily lives. Living in relationship with the Holy Spirit allows us to break and tear down the control of the spirits of this world,

---

80 John 20:21, NIV.

81 John 14:18, NIV.

82 Luke Timothy Johnson. *The Creed: What Christians Believe and Why It Matters*, (New York, Image/Doubleday Press, 2003), p. 221-223. "Power" (Romans 15:13), it "leads" (Romans 8:14), it "testifies" (Acts 20:23), it "makes known" (1 Peter 1:11) , it "drives Jesus to the wilderness" (Mark 1:2), it "speaks"(1 Timothy 4:1), it is the "advocate" and the "comforter" (John 14:16).

83 Migliore, p. 228.

84 Acts 2 and Acts 3.

85 Matthew 16:18, NIV.

and allows our lives to be transformed by the power of the living God through the Holy Spirit. The same power of the Holy Spirit is available to us as believers as was available to those first Christians who experienced the Holy Spirit as transformational in their lives. "I, too, can allow the Holy Spirit to touch my life personally with the personal presence of God that exists through the resurrection of Jesus Christ."[86]

The Holy Spirit is associated with fruit, and the one that bestows gifts of the Holy Spirit. The *gifts* are given by the Spirit for the purpose of building up the community of the body of Christ—the church! They are given to all believers so that the kingdom in this world might be built up. The *fruit* are the results of the Holy Spirit acting in a believer's life.

Theologian Kendall Soulen puts it well when he states that the gift of the Holy Spirit is a gift of new life. "The Holy Spirit brings people in unity with each other in a way that plants the seed of eternal life and replaces spirits that are distorted in relation to God."[87] It is the first fruit or the down payment in the present for the realization of the fullness of eternal life in the world to come. The work of the Holy Spirit is beginning to do in us what God has already accomplished in Jesus Christ. When I grow in the work of the Holy Spirit I look forward to the full realization of that which is already realized in Jesus Christ on behalf of me, the church, and ultimately on behalf of the world as a whole. The fullness of the work of the Holy Spirit is fully realized with the world to come.

Peter and other believers were being empowered by the Holy Spirit to birth the church. The church is not a human invention or human driven, but rather, the church is empowered by the Holy Spirit, and the very gates of Hell will not overcome it! We the people *are* the church. The church is not four walls with a pretty steeple, the church is not an historic building, but rather the church is the Body of Christ, empowered by the Holy Spirit, to be on the move for the purpose of making disciples. We are empowered for the purpose of continuing to usher in the kingdom of God. To be effective, we need to understand that it is imperative to share our God stories. Our actions are not enough, we must use words, too.

The Holy Spirit creates a community in which there is something new that was not here before. We are all united as part of the body of Christ in this new community—called the church, which is created for the purpose of transformation of the larger community and of the world around us. This is part of the realized change as a result of the life, death, and resurrection of Christ here on earth. This is part of the new community. This community called church has access to the transformational power and authority of the Holy Spirit, and it lives under the authority of the Spirit, upon which Christ is the cornerstone.

Peter began forming this new community by sharing God stories. His speeches started with the story of Jesus, then Peter explained how we each are saved through the resurrection of Jesus the Christ. In each case, the listeners recognized Peter and the other disciples were "unschooled, ordinary men," and the rulers, elders, and teachers of the law were astonished at their teaching, and at the performing of miracles.[88] Peter becomes more bodacious when the leaders of the church tell him to stop talking about Jesus. The reply from John and Peter, "Which is right in God's eyes: to listen to you, or to him [Jesus]? You be the judges! As for us, we cannot help speaking about what we have seen and heard."[89]

---

86 Johnson, p. 223.
87 Soulen, Systematic Lecture Notes 3/9/06.
88 Acts 4:13, NIV.
89 Acts 4: 19-20, NIV.

The power these men and women had in sharing their God stories should not surprise us. This has been part of God's plan all along. Beginning with God's promise to Abraham, we have seen that God had a purpose for God's chosen people from the beginning of time. This was a plan that the world and all its inhabitants would come to know the God who created, the God who saves, and the God who sustains us in life. The technical term for this plan is the *Missio Dei*. *Missio Dei* is a Latin theological term that can be translated as "Mission of God." The term refers to the work of the church as being part of God's work. The church's mission is a subset of a larger whole mission that it is both part of God's mission to the world and not the entirety of God's work in reconciling and transforming this broken world.[90]

Theologian Leslie Newbigin suggests that, "The trinitarian nature of mission implies an important role for the church. Communication and community lies at the heart of the trinity and therefore must lie at the heart of trinitarian mission. The call to conversion is a call to become part of a community called the church, and *Missio Dei* comes from that community."[91] Other missiologists remind us that, "Both the church and the mission of the church are tools of God, instruments through which God carries out this mission." "Mission is therefore seen as a movement from God to the world. The church is viewed as an instrument for that mission." In this view, the whole purpose of the church is to support the *Missio Dei* and church structures exist in order to serve the community in mission.[92]

Interest in mission and the sharing of our God stories is declining in many of our churches. Part of this decline is the nature of the post-modern mindset which sees all human narratives as being of equal value and importance. In our Western culture, sometimes we are afraid to share our God stories because others believe that all narratives, all stories, are of equal value. While each person is of equal value and of sacred worth, God's story trumps personal opinion. Our existence begins with God. "*Missio Dei* not only provides a theological key for mission in a post-modern age, it also provides a motivational factor for us when we struggle with the challenges of post-modernism, pluralism and globalization. In our current cultural context, Christians have become reluctant to 'impose' their views on others."[93]

Missio Dei elevates mission above the level of human activities, and shows us that mission is actually participation in something which God is already doing. Sharing our God stories is therefore no longer elevating one human opinion over and above another equally valid one. Rather, sharing our God stories becomes something that is at the very heart of who we were created to be as children of God and inheritors of the promise. There is a clear divine sanction for mission and evangelism—in short, sharing our God stories becomes the principle *raison d'être* of the church.[94] Sharing our God stories is what we were created to do.

God is a sending God, and God, in turn, sends us. Missiologist David J. Bosch reports, "Mission is not primarily an activity of the church, but an attribute of God. God is a missionary God."[95] If our God sent God's Son, and in turn the Son and the Father sent the Holy Spirit, are we really thinking God will not in turn send us? Not only does God send us, but God sends us through the church, because, as it has been said, "While the church might be flawed, it is the best means we have for carrying out the *Missio Dei* of God."[96] The people of the church are empowered by God to move forward in order to carry out this

90 www.wikipedia.org, accessed May 5, 2015.

91 Leslie Newbigin, *The Open Secret: An Introduction to the Theology of Mission.* (London, SPCK, 1995), p. 76.

92 *Eddie Arthur,* http://www.wycliffe.net/resources/missiology/globalperspectives/tabid/97/Default.aspx?id=3960, accessed May 5, 2015.

93 R. Dowsett, *Dry Bones in the West,* in Global Missiology for 21st Century: Reflections from the Iguassu Dialogue, ed. W. D. Taylor. (Grand Rapids, IL, Baker Academic, 2001), p. 449.

94 *Eddie Arthur,* http://www.wycliffe.net/resources/missiology/globalperspectives/tabid/97/Default.aspx?id=3960, accessed May 5, 2015.

95 David J. Bosch, *Transforming Mission: Paradigm Shifts in Theology of Mission* (Maryknoll, NY, OrbisBooks, 1991), p. 420.

96 This has been stated so many times that it is fairly well universally used at this point in time.

mission. The mission is to make disciples for Jesus, and it is carried out through continuing to tell our God stories, and continuing to be part of the building of the kingdom of God on earth as it is in heaven.

The *Missio Dei* of God is the reason we share our God stories. We have often forgotten that we are a people, sent by God to bless the nations. We can bless the nations by sharing our God stories. This is the purpose of the church. This is the purpose of each individual who calls themselves Christian. This is God's mission, and therefore it is our mission, too!

SMALL GROUP LEADER DISCUSSION - WEEK FIVE

1. What does empowered by the Holy Spirit mean to you? Have you ever been empowered by the Holy Spirit? Can you describe a time when the Holy Spirit gave power or ability greater than your own power or ability? Do you think the Holy Spirit still empowers us today as the Holy Spirit empowered the believers of the early church?

   a. What does culture say about this?

   b. What do other Christians say?

   c. What does the Bible say?

2. Compare Peter's speeches in Acts 2:14-41, Acts 3:11-26, and Acts 4:8-21. What do you find different and what seems to be the same? What was powerful about his witness? What did he always include in his story telling? What was left out?

3. Have you heard of the term "*Missio Dei*" before? What are your thoughts of God being a missionary God? Does this ring true to you?

4. When have you seized the opportunity, like Peter, to be a bold witness for Jesus?

5. What is the purpose of the church?

   a. What does culture say about the purpose of the church?

   b. What do other Christians say?

   c. What does the Bible say?

   d. Do you think these purposes match God's view of the Body of Christ?

6. Is the contemporary church responding to the brokenness of the world in effective ways?

7. What do you think is the primary reason for the sharing of our God stories?

DAILY DEVOTIONALS - WEEK FIVE

SHARING YOUR STORY - THE CHURCH - BOLD AND BODACIOUS

DAY 1   **THE PROMISE.**   **ACTS 2:14, 39**

"Then Peter stood up with the Eleven, raised his voice and addressed the crowd, 'Fellow Jews and all of you who live in Jerusalem, let me explain this to you; listen carefully to what I say.'" Verse 14, NIV *"The promise is for you and your children and for all who are far off—for all whom the Lord our God will call."* Verse 39, NIV

It is impossible to talk about the promise of God and our relationship with God without connecting it to our own relationship with the parents or guardians in our own lives or those whom we parent or guard. Regardless of the structure of the relationship, adult/child relationships are fraught with promises. Maybe we didn't pinky swear or cross our hearts and hope to die, maybe we didn't spit into our hands and shake on it, or give a Boy Scouts hand sign, but promises are made all the time. And the truth is, some promises we keep, some we do not, some we make knowing we can never fulfill, others we spend our entire lives trying to fill. Some promises require great sacrifice, some sacrifices make it too hard to keep the promise.

But regardless of the outcome of the promise made, I would like to believe that every promise is made not out of obligation or expectation, but simply out of love. For it is the same love that God has for you and me and that flows from us to others. For *the promise is for you, for your children, and for all who are far away, everyone whom the Lord our God calls to him."* (Acts 2:39, NRSV) What was that promise? This week we will look at those promises as Peter begins his apostolic ministry preaching the good news of a Resurrected Christ. What we will discover is that all these promises are made possible by the death, burial, and resurrection of Jesus Christ. These are promises that have never been broken and are still being fulfilled.

Reflection: What promise has God made to you? What promise have you made to others? What can you do this week to be as true to your promise as God has been to God's promise?

Prayer: Dear Lord, I thank you for keeping your promise of life abundant in Christ and life eternal with Christ. Help me to be as faithful to you and others in keeping my promise to be a faithful disciple of Jesus Christ in the world today. Amen. -Rev. Dr. Michelle Holmes Chaney

DAILY DEVOTIONALS - WEEK FIVE

SHARING YOUR STORY - THE CHURCH - BOLD AND BODACIOUS

DAY 2   **THE PROMISE OF THE HOLY SPIRIT.**   **ACTS 2:14-21**

"Then Peter stood up with the Eleven, raised his voice and addressed the crowd: 'Fellow Jews and all of you who live in Jerusalem, let me explain this to you; listen carefully to what I say. These people are not drunk, as you suppose. It's only nine in the morning! No, this is what was spoken by the prophet Joel: 'In the last days, God says, I will pour out my Spirit on all people. Your sons and daughters will prophesy, your young men will see visions, your old men will dream dreams. Even on my servants, both men and women, I will pour out my Spirit in those days, and they will prophesy. I will show wonders in the heavens above and signs on the earth below, blood and fire and billows of smoke. The sun will be turned to darkness and the moon to blood before the coming of the great and glorious day of the Lord. And everyone who calls on the name of the Lord will be saved.'" NIV

"Didn't I tell you that would happen?" Those familiar words in the voice of my grandmother, still echo in my ear. Even though she died when I was nine years old, her spirit still speaks to me when I need to hear her, and I can see her standing in front of me, hand on hip, finger pointing.

Peter stands before the crowd and reminds them that what they are experiencing is exactly what Jesus said would happen. He promised the disciples that the Holy Spirit would come as Jesus spent his last hours with them.[97] And the promise was kept when he met with them in the upper room as they began their ministry as apostles.[98] Peter also reminds them that Jesus said that while John baptized with water, they would be baptized with the Holy Spirit.[99] And now he must remind them that the promise of the Holy Spirit was part of God's plan all along in recounting Joel's prophesy.[100]

And now we have an Advocate, a Friend, a Confidant, a Wise Sage, a Guide to remind us who we are and whose we are, in Christ Jesus.

Reflection: Think about a time when the Holy Spirit was clearly present with you as an Advocate, a Friend, a Confidant, a Wise Sage, or a Guide. What were the circumstances? How was it resolved? Could you have come to that resolution on your own? Why or why not?

Prayer: Dear Lord, thank you for the gift of your Holy Spirit. As we grow as your disciples, our desire is to increase in our reliance on your Spirit to direct our lives as we share our God stories and reach out to those who still do not know you. Amen. -Rev. Dr. Michelle Holmes Chaney

---

97 John 14: 15-17, NIV.
98 John 20:19-23, NIV.
99 Acts 1:4-5, NIV.
100 Acts 2:17-21, NIV

SHARING YOUR STORY - THE CHURCH - BOLD AND BODACIOUS

DAY 3   **THE PROMISE OF SALVATION.**   **ACTS 2:40-47**

"With many other words he warned them; and he pleaded with them, 'Save yourselves from this corrupt generation.' Those who accepted his message were baptized, and about three thousand were added to their number that day. They devoted themselves to the apostles' teaching and to fellowship, to the breaking of bread and to prayer. Everyone was filled with awe at the many wonders and signs performed by the apostles. All the believers were together and had everything in common. They sold property and possessions to give to anyone who had need. Every day they continued to meet together in the temple courts. They broke bread in their homes and ate together with glad and sincere hearts, praising God and enjoying the favor of all the people. And the Lord added to their number daily those who were being saved." NIV

This past Christmas Eve my husband and I were asked to serve communion at a noon day service designed to accompany a Christmas luncheon for the homeless that live in and around the downtown area. Because a large crowd was expected, the church chose to use communion wafers rather than serving baked bread. As we were serving, an older gentleman took the wafer from me, looked at it, smelled it, flicked it with his other hand, shook his head and handed the wafer back to me and walked off. Clearly something that made the server and me both chuckle during the car ride home. This encounter got me thinking about John Wesley's Sermon 101: *The Duty of Constant Communion,* where Wesley saw Communion not as an obligation but as an opportunity to "remember" the sacrifice made by Jesus so that we might receive the promise of salvation. In fact, it is our unworthiness and need for salvation that should draw us to the Lord's table. We all need to be reminded that the Lord's table is not for the perfect, but for those who accept the promise.

Reflection: Reflect on the service of communion where you worship. Is it truly inviting? To you? To others? What would make it even more inviting?

Prayer: Dear Lord, we are thankful that we are welcome at your table. Help us to make more room, not just at your table, but in our hearts, for those who need to know the promise of salvation. Empower us to not only share our God stories, but to also break bread together in the name of Jesus. Amen. -Rev. Dr. Michelle Holmes Chaney

DAILY DEVOTIONALS - WEEK FIVE

SHARING YOUR STORY - THE CHURCH - BOLD AND BODACIOUS

DAY 4   **THE PROMISE OF HEALING AND HEALTH.**   **ACTS 3:1-10**

"One day Peter and John were going up to the temple at the time of prayer—at three in the afternoon. Now a man who was lame from birth was being carried to the temple gate called Beautiful, where he was put every day to beg from those going into the temple courts. When he saw Peter and John about to enter, he asked them for money. Peter looked straight at him, as did John. Then Peter said, 'Look at us!' So the man gave them his attention, expecting to get something from them. Then Peter said, 'Silver or gold I do not have, but what I do have I give you. In the name of Jesus Christ of Nazareth, walk.' Taking him by the right hand, he helped him up, and instantly the man's feet and ankles became strong. He jumped to his feet and began to walk. Then he went with them into the temple courts, walking and jumping, and praising God. When all the people saw him walking and praising God, they recognized him as the same man who used to sit begging at the temple gate called Beautiful, and they were filled with wonder and amazement at what had happened to him." NIV

Perhaps you have heard the old saying from the Spanish philosopher Maimonides, "Give a man a fish and you feed him for a day, teach a man to fish and you feed him for a lifetime." I am not much for fishing, but I have come to appreciate that particular saying in light of working with people who are in need. Sometimes they are so in need that they no longer know what they really need. I believe it is for us as disciples of Jesus Christ to be able to discern the real need, through the power of the Holy Spirit, and find a way to address that need.

We encounter Peter and John faced with the same need for discernment. They encounter a man who wanted alms, Peter offered healing so he could support himself. We see this same story at the Pool by the Sheep Gate when Jesus asks the paralyzed man, "Do you want to be made well?"[101] The man wanted to be out in the pool, Jesus wanted to heal the man so he would not have to depend on others again. In both instances, focusing on the long term and not the moment creates an opportunity to point to Jesus Christ and his power to heal. Addressing the real need creates real opportunity for relationship with Jesus Christ, and the promise of healing.

Reflection: Are there situations in your life where you want Jesus to apply a "quick fix," but Jesus is trying to get you to accept the promise of healing? What do you need to do differently to accept the promise?

Prayer: Dear Lord, help me to seek you for the healing that only you can provide. I accept your promise of healing and pray for courage and strength to move into your promise every day. Amen. -Rev. Dr. Michelle Holmes Chaney

---

101 John 5:6, NIV.

DAILY DEVOTIONALS - WEEK FIVE

SHARING YOUR STORY - THE CHURCH - BOLD AND BODACIOUS

DAY 5   **THE PROMISE OF REPENTANCE.**   **ACTS 3:17-20**

"Now, fellow Israelites, I know that you acted in ignorance, as did your leaders. But this is how God fulfilled what he had foretold through all the prophets, saying that his Messiah would suffer. Repent, then, and turn to God, so that your sins may be wiped out, that times of refreshing may come from the Lord, and that he may send the Messiah, who has been appointed for you—even Jesus." NIV

Many years ago, my brother and I were horsing around in our New York apartment. We were home from school, and clearly we were getting bored. My brother got the bright idea to dress up and pretend to be a sword fighter. He put on a costume that looked more like a pirate than a sword fighter, whatever that is, and he went into the kitchen and came back with my mother's longest and sharpest knife, reserved for cutting holiday meats. As I sat on the sofa he jumped from chair to sofa to loveseat all the while swinging that knife. Well, one swing too many and my brother managed to cut the lampshade and the window shade behind it in half. Clear that this could not end well, my brother promised me five dollars if I said I stumbled and fell into the table the lamp sat on and caused it to fall over and rip the lampshade, taking the window shade with it. I am guessing you know how this went down...fast forward many hours and my mother is reciting all the chores my brother would have to do over the next two weeks to make up for what he had done. And when she said to him, "You could have cut your sister's head off!" he just looked at me and said, "But I didn't!"

Repentance is no small matter for us as children of God. In this text, Peter reminds his "friends" that repentance is important not only to have your "sins wiped out" but also that "times of refreshing may come from the presence of the Lord."[102]   Peter spoke boldly to those who had a hand in Jesus' death in the hopes that they would repent. Sometimes we need to speak boldly to our own sin and seek to repent; seek to *really* repent.

Reflection: We all have sins for which we need forgiveness and repentance. Recall a time when repentance was most difficult for you. How did you overcome it?

Prayer: Dear Lord, sin has separated me from you, and repentance has blocked the road to my return. Help me to be ever aware of my sin, and challenge me to live a life of not only forgiveness, but also repentance. In the name of Jesus Christ I pray, Amen. -Rev. Dr. Michelle Holmes Chaney

---

102 Acts 3:19-20, NIV.

DAILY DEVOTIONALS - WEEK FIVE

SHARING YOUR STORY - THE CHURCH - BOLD AND BODACIOUS

DAY 6   **THE PROMISE OF REJECTION.**   **ACTS 4:8-13**

"Then Peter, filled with the Holy Spirit, said to them, 'Rulers and elders of the people! If we are being called to account today for an act of kindness shown to a man who was lame and are being asked how he was healed, then know this, you and all the people of Israel: It is by the name of Jesus Christ of Nazareth, whom you crucified but whom God raised from the dead, that this man stands before you healed. Jesus is the stone you builders rejected, which has become the cornerstone. Salvation is found in no one else, for there is no other name under heaven given to mankind by which we must be saved.' When they saw the courage of Peter and John and realized that they were unschooled, ordinary men, they were astonished and they took note that these men had been with Jesus." NIV

The thought of rejection is crippling. The same is true following through with an act that could lead to rejection. That is why some Christians struggle with sharing the story of Jesus Christ with others. Their first thought is, "What if they do not want to listen? What if they do not like what I say?" Jesus was no stranger to rejection. Rejection is the reason Jesus was killed in the first place. But while our call is to be 'like' Christ, there are many things Christ did on which we would rather take a pass. Part of our human development is learning to accept and cope with rejection. It starts when we do not get picked to be on a team for a game of softball, and goes all the way to not getting elected to be President of the United States. Peter accepted rejection, for it confirmed to him that he was walking in Jesus' path.

Reflection: With such a wonderful role model in Jesus, we should know how to deal with rejection, and the answer to dealing with rejection is not avoidance. We, too, must learn to face the rejection head on, knowing we cannot take it personally. For, what others reject is not our story of how much Jesus loves us. They reject the thought that Jesus could love them just as much!

Prayer: Jesus, you are not only our savior, but you are also our model and our mentor. Help us to tap into the Holy Ghost's boldness just as your first apostles did, and empower us to be more willing to accept rejection in the hopes that someone will be saved. Amen. -Rev. Dr. Michelle Holmes Chaney

DAILY DEVOTIONALS - WEEK FIVE

SHARING YOUR STORY - THE CHURCH - BOLD AND BODACIOUS

DAY 7   **THE PROMISE OF THE LORD'S COMING.**   **2 PETER 3:9**

"The Lord is not slow in keeping his promise, as some understand slowness. Instead he is patient with you, not wanting anyone to perish, but everyone to come to repentance." NIV

When I was in my twenties, I thought I had all the time in the world. Now that I am in my fifties, I still think I have all the time in the world, I just want to be way more productive with my time! The truth is, the only one who has all the time in the world is God. And because Jesus does not want any of us to spend eternity dead in sin and not alive with Him, Jesus remains patient, planning his triumphant return to earth, but never wanting to jump the gun. Instead being patient, "not willing that any should perish, but that all should come to repentance." (2 Peter 3:9) KJV. That kind of repentance is challenging to imagine even on our best days.

Reflection: What promises have you made to God? How are you living out those promises as a believer in Jesus Christ and as a disciple for the transformation of the world?

Prayer: Jesus, you are the manifestation of God's promise to us. We thank you that you became flesh and dwelt among us. Help us live transformed lives as we seek to transform lives for you. Empower us to have a holy boldness in sharing our God stories so that others might come to know your saving grace. In Jesus' name we pray. Amen. -Rev. Dr. Michelle Holmes Chaney

SERMON OUTLINE - WEEK FIVE

SHARING YOUR STORY - THE CHURCH - BOLD AND BODACIOUS

ACTS 2:29-33; ACTS 3:11-21; OR ACTS 4

1. Friday was a big day in celebration of the 70th anniversary of victory from WW2. (Choose some local victory that has been recently celebrated. This fit into the time line I used.)

    a. Vintage World War II planes flew down the National Mall.

    b. More than 50 military planes in 15 formations made their way down the Potomac River to the Lincoln Memorial and down Independence Avenue to the House office buildings before returning to airports in Culpeper and Manassas, Va.

    c. They flew in sequenced formations recounting the biggest battles of World War II, from Pearl Harbor to the final assault on Japan.

2. I saw it on TV, but the fly over represented a sharing of a story, a story that is larger than us, but represented by those planes, flying in victory formation.

    a. We are grateful for those who took part in the victory.

        i. I still remember Mr. Guy, one of our former parishioners, telling us his account of D-Day. He had been there, and came out alive.

        ii. We become part of bigger stories, stories that formed the very fabric of the earth in which we live.

3. That is the way it is with God's story.

    a. God's intersection in our lives becomes a part of our stories.

    b. Becomes part of the fabric of who you are.

    c. Just as the WWII vets want to share their stories, and we want to hear, so too, we want to share the stories of how God has intersected with human lives, and how we have felt God's presence with us.

    d. As you have your own God experiences, you also want to share those stories with others, so that they too, might benefit from your experience.

        i. Just as we want to share in the victory of WWII, even though most of us were not present, so too we want to share in the victory of Christ, the victory of Christ overcoming death through the miraculous Easter Resurrection.

        ii. God has embedded in the very DNA of our lives the need be a part of the one who created us, a part of what God is doing.

        iii. We learn what God is doing by sharing our stories.

            1. Those stories can be about many things.

                a. That experience we share may be about how God empowered us to overcome adversity.

                b. Or, a near death experience.

                c. It might be a story of adventure that changed us and empowered us to recognize that God is active in our lives.

SERMON OUTLINE - WEEK FIVE

4. Just as the end of WWII was a world changing event, so too, and even more so, was the resurrection of Jesus.

    a. The resurrection changed everything, brought new life, new hope, new victories.

    b. It gave us, as humans, a way to know that God is near.

        i. It gave us freedom at the cross to know our sins are forgiven, that we are no longer enslaved to sin.

        ii. It empowers us to be new creations in Christ Jesus.

        iii. And it gives us the desire to follow Jesus, to allow Jesus to be our Lord.

        iv. Hearing God stories from other people invites us to be in a life changing relationship with Jesus.

    c. Accepting Christ should become a life changing event for us.

    d. John Wesley calls it, "The heart strangely warmed."

    e. You know that Jesus is with you.

    f. You know that nothing can ever separate you from Christ.

5. If accepting Jesus as Lord becomes our story, should that story not become a story that we continually want to share?

    a. The story of victory in WWII, is a story that the vets never tire of sharing.

    b. That story becomes part of the fabric that defines them.

        i. So too, our God stories should define who we are, and we should be sharing them over and over again.

6. Many of you are aware that this is week 5 of a 7 week series entitled, Sharing Your God Story.

    a. Here is a quick review: We have seen how God blesses for the purpose of us sharing that blessing.

    b. We see God continually calling back God's people and making a way for them to be back in right relationship with God.

        i. Even when the people sin and turn away.

        ii. Last week we ultimately saw that Jesus came to give us a new way of salvation as he offered his own life on the cross in exchange for our lives of sin.

        iii. We saw Jesus offer presence and compassion.

        iv. We saw Jesus listening to the stories of others and modeling a new way for his disciples.

        v. Remember when we saw the resurrected Jesus go up in the clouds. That was called the Ascension. Before he left, he told his disciples to go make disciples.

        vi. Jesus told his disciples, "As the father is sending me, so I am sending you."

        vii. Last week we learned that we ourselves are to be a sent people.

        viii. But how do we share those God stories, with whom do we share them, and how do we do it?

7. For our biblical guide this day we have Peter, the disciple of Jesus.

SERMON OUTLINE - WEEK FIVE

 a. Remember Peter fell asleep when Jesus was praying in Gethsemane; Peter denied Jesus; and Peter ran away when Jesus was crucified.

 b. Yet this same man, who denied Jesus for fear of being killed himself, was empowered to tell his story.

 c. How? By the power of the Holy Spirit that fell upon the disciples on the day of Pentecost.

  i. You might recall that Jesus said, "I have to go away in order for the helper, the advocate, the *paracletos* to come."

  ii. Jesus was referring to the third person of the Trinity, the Holy Spirit.

8. Who is the person of the Holy Spirit?

 a. The one who sustains us in life, the one who corrects, guides, continues the ministry that Jesus began here on earth...with one big difference.

 b. For those who believe in Jesus, the Holy Spirit resides in you, and it empowers.

  i. The day of Pentecost is the day we celebrate the birth of the church, for it is the day the Holy Spirit empowered God's people to be more, to do more, to be the reflection of God on earth, as it is in heaven.

   1. This is the day the Church was born.

   2. Jesus called Peter out to lead it. How? Through the power of the Holy Spirit.

 c. We are empowered by the Holy Spirit, which is the reason Peter could stand in front of the very people who sentenced Jesus to death, and tell the story of Jesus.

9. Listen to how Peter and the others were empowered by the Spirit—to birth the church.

 a. This is Peter the denier, now bold and bodacious. (This means excellent, admirable, or attractive.)

 b. First, he tells the story of Jesus and the resurrection.

  i. Notice, he starts where the people are: The Jews' most famous leader was King David, so he begins with their most faith filled leader, and moves forward from there.

   1. "Fellow Israelites, I can tell you confidently that the patriarch David died and was buried, and his tomb is here to this day. But he was a prophet and knew that God had promised him on oath that he would place one of his descendants on his throne. Seeing what was to come, he spoke of the resurrection of the Messiah, that he was not abandoned to the realm of the dead, nor did his body see decay. God has raised this Jesus to life, and we are all witnesses of it. Exalted to the right hand of God, he has received from the Father the promised Holy Spirit and has poured out what you now see and hear... Therefore let all Israel be assured of this: God has made this Jesus, whom you crucified, both Lord and Messiah... Peter replied, 'Repent and be baptized, every one of you, in the name of Jesus Christ for the forgiveness of your sins. And you will receive the gift of the Holy Spirit. The promise is for you and your children and for all who are far off—for all whom the Lord our God will call!'"

   2. Don't miss this promise, the promise is for you and your children. (Remember our sermon a couple of weeks ago, God's promise will NOT come back empty.)

    ii.   So Peter was telling them that this Jesus was bigger than David.

    iii.   The people then asked, "What must we then do?" The next verse says, "They were cut to the heart."

        1.   Peter tells them, repent and be baptized...see even if you participated in the death of this Jesus, there is forgiveness, repent and be baptized.

            a.   That is a pretty big forgiveness package right there.

10. In the next chapter Peter continues to tell God's story through the lens of the history of the Israelites and the current events. (Notice none of this could happen unless they were empowered by the Holy Spirit.)

    a.   Peter and John were going into the temple. They see a lame beggar.

    b.   These are the famous words from Peter, "Silver or gold I do not have, but what I do have I give you. In the name of Jesus Christ of Nazareth, walk."

    c.   And the man miraculously walks. We pick up Acts 3, verse 11:

        i.   "While the man held on to Peter and John, all the people were astonished and came running to them in the place called Solomon's Colonnade. When Peter saw this, he said to them: 'Fellow Israelites, why does this surprise you? Why do you stare at us as if by our own power or godliness we had made this man walk? The God of Abraham, Isaac and Jacob, the God of our fathers, has glorified his servant Jesus. You handed him over to be killed, and you disowned him before Pilate, though he had decided to let him go. You disowned the Holy and Righteous One and asked that a murderer be released to you. You killed the author of life, but God raised him from the dead. We are witnesses of this. By faith in the name of Jesus, this man whom you see and know was made strong. It is Jesus' name and the faith that comes through him that has completely healed him, as you can all see.

            'Now, fellow Israelites, I know that you acted in ignorance, as did your leaders. But this is how God fulfilled what he had foretold through all the prophets, saying that his Messiah would suffer. Repent, then, and turn to God, so that your sins may be wiped out, that times of refreshing may come from the Lord, and that he may send the Messiah, who has been appointed for you—even Jesus.'"

11. Once again, Peter uses the platform of current events to tell the story of Jesus, and offer forgiveness of sins, through the power of Jesus. (Tie this story into the current event story used at the beginning.)

    a.   This is the stuff that authentic stories are made of.

    b.   This is the stuff that people relate to.

        i.   Can you imagine when every person saw this man, and asked, "How is it you can now walk?"

            1.   And he responds, "Well there were these guys, and they said they knew Jesus who was crucified, but then came back from the dead.

            2.   And they said in his name I can walk, and it happened."

12. Our united common history and current events empower us to tell stories.

    a.   Just as we like to hear the stories of vets who changed history.

    b. So too, people want to hear stories of Jesus that are relevant to their lives, stories of Jesus changing lives.

          i. The vets were eye witnesses.

          ii. The apostles were eye witnesses.

          iii. While you and I were not eye witnesses, we have these stories handed down from one generation of believers to the next.

          iv. Hence the reason it is called apostolic ministry, it goes from one teacher to the next teacher.

13. So how can you unite your own story and a current event to share a God story?

    a. What would that look like for you?

          i. First you have to discover and be able to tell one aspect of your own God story.

              1. Was there something that brought you back to church?

              2. Was there a time you were at rock bottom and you recognized that Jesus created you for more than this?

              3. Was there a time that a stranger spoke hope into you, as Peter did for the lame beggar?

    b. Here are some key themes to look for in life intersections for people's lives, because it is often during a life intersection that people want to hear about God. (Graduations, new jobs, weddings, funerals, birth of a baby, divorce, sickness, unwanted news such as cancer).

          i. Hope, joy, frustration, lack of forgiveness, new life, transformation, down in depths, life chaos, life worries.

          ii. Change is the key, change at life's intersections.

          iii. These are times people are most vulnerable and most likely to listen to a God story that will speak truth into their lives.

14. Here is the deal:

    a. In the words of Jesus, "As the Father has sent me, so I too, send you."

    b. This phrase is often referred to as the *Missio Dei*, or the mission of God.

    c. **This doctrine, or teaching of the universal church, reminds us that just as God is a sending God, sending Jesus, and the father and Jesus sending the Spirit, so, too, we are a sent people.**

    d. What are we sent for?

          i. To share the good news of Jesus.

          ii. To tell our stories.

          iii. To offer joy and hope and peace in the name of Jesus.

    e. Why does Jesus send us?

          i. It's not that God cannot do this by God's own self.

          ii. God wants us to be a part of what God is doing.

          iii. This is how we build relationship with God.

    iv.   Sharing our God stories brings us in a deeper relationship with God.

    v.   So there is a twofold process:

        1.   Sharing our stories brings us closer to others.

        2.   Sharing our stories brings us closer to God.

15. Maybe you are sitting here thinking, well, that is nice pastor, but it is just not me.

    a.   Did you not hear Peter's story?

    b.   Peter was a guy who was fully scared before the crucifixion.

        i.   He talked a big talk, but when push came to shove, he denied Jesus, which caused him to weep bitterly.

        ii.   Then he left—he ran away.

        iii.   And he was nowhere to be seen at the crucifixion.

        iv.   Then, this same guy was empowered by the Holy Spirit.

        v.   And this same guy was chosen by Jesus to lead the church.

            1.   To be bold and bodacious.

16. Friends, we too, are empowered by the Spirit for more than what we can do on our own.

    a.   Miracles and healings were not just for the days after the resurrection of Jesus.

    b.   The Holy Spirit continues to empower us in ways beyond our own human ability.

        i.   Healing takes place in many shapes and forms.

        ii.   So, too, empowerment by the Spirit takes many shapes and forms.

        iii.   One shape is by giving us the correct words when we do not have the words to say.

            1.   On more than one occasion I have been places where I did not have the words, the words that came out were those of the Spirit.

            2.   Often stories that are told to me are those that people said, "I had no idea what to say, and then the words just came, they were not my words."

            3.   Those, my friends, are the words of the Holy Spirit.

        iv.   We are told that the Holy Spirit resides in us, and there is power for those who believe in the name of Jesus.

        v.   Invite the Holy Spirit to be present in you, around you, and through you.

        vi.   Have courage to be part of what God is doing in other people's lives.

        vii.   Allow God to use your part of God's story.

17. Just like the WWII stories are powerful to remind us of the cost of freedom for our country, so too our God stories remind us of the cost of the redemption given to us by Jesus on the cross.

    a.   You might not think you have a story, but you have one.

    b.   Search it out, tell it to a trusted friend, practice telling it.

    c.   Invite God, through the power of the Holy Spirit, to use you in a profound way.

      i.   My joy will be to hear your story.

     ii.   In how God used you to tell your story, and offer hope, to someone who crossed your path, who needed to hear that there is new life through Jesus Christ.

18. So go forward, knowing that the Holy Spirit will guide you. Offer yourselves to God to use you in sharing your God stories.

Amen.

LITURGY FOR WORSHIP - WEEK FIVE

SHARING YOUR STORY - THE CHURCH - BOLD AND BODACIOUS

FIRST SCRIPTURE READING: ACTS 2:29-33

READING BEFORE THE SERMON: ACTS 3:11-21

CALL TO WORSHIP: (based on Acts 3)
Gathered as your community we call upon the name of Jesus to transform us.
By faith in the name of Jesus we have been made strong.
Gathered as your people, we can do all things through the name of Jesus and the power of your Holy Spirit.
By faith in the name of Jesus we have been empowered.
Gathered as your people, we are the body of Christ, the Church, and we can transform the world.
By faith in the name of Jesus we have become your hands, feet, and voice.
Let us move out into the world as your people, your church, the bride of Christ.

PRAYER OF CONFESSION:
Sending God, too often we forget that we are a sent people. Sometimes we get things backwards and think that the church belongs to us, forgetting that the church is your bride. Remind us, Lord, that you created us for community so that we could be your agents of change in the world. Remind us that even as you are in the process of transforming us, you also use us to transform the world. Empower us by your Holy Spirit to share our God stories, so that others might have the hope that is in you. Amen.

POSSIBLE HYMNS:
2120   Spirit, Spirit of Gentleness
2118   Holy Spirit, Come to Us, (Taize)
2124   Come, O Holy Spirit, Come
558   We Are the Church
545   The Church's One Foundation
593   Here I Am Lord

* *Three digit page numbers refer to the United Methodist Hymnal*
* *Four digit page numbers refer to The Faith We Sing Hymnal*

POSSIBLE PRAISE SONGS:
Oceans by Hillsong United
Build Your Kingdom Here by Rend Collective
Lay Me Down by Chris Tomlin
Waterfall by Chris Tomlin
You Make Me Brave by Elevation Worship
Forever Reign by Hillsong United

Week Six
The Church -
Moving Beyond Comfort Zones

What is your story?

SMALL GROUP LEADER - WEEK SIX

SHARING YOUR STORY - MOVING BEYOND COMFORT ZONES

In the previous chapter we encountered the Holy Spirit empowering believers to tell their God stories for the purpose of making new disciples for Jesus and ushering in the new creation, the kingdom of God. The Holy Spirit makes itself known in the biblical drama as the means by which God gives life. Paul writes, "If the Spirit of him who raised Jesus from the dead dwells in you, he who raised Christ from the dead will give life to your mortal bodies also through his Spirit that dwells in you."[103] The Holy Spirit is the spirit that brings new life in situations where the community has turned away from the possibility of life. The Holy Spirit extends the possibility of new life when a creature or a community, such as Israel, or the church, has run out of the possibility of new life. The same thing is true when Jesus Christ ran out of physical life; it was the work of the Holy Spirit that raised Jesus Christ up in resurrection. When we are dead in sin and destruction, it is the Holy Spirit that truly brings new life.[104]

The disciples were empowered by this same Spirit to begin faith communities which we know as the church. The purpose of the church is to be the community that proclaims who God is and what God has done in God's created world. The Book of Discipline of The United Methodist Church states that, "The mission of the church is to make disciples of Jesus Christ. The local churches provide the most significant arena through which disciple making occurs."[105] This community called church, while imperfect, is the best way we have of living out the gospel message.

This idea of church community is critical to the ongoing mission of God, the *Missio Dei*. Remember that the church was God's idea, it is not of human origin. Those who say, "I believe in Jesus, but I do not believe in organized religion" are acting contrary to biblical teaching. It is the faith community that continues to usher in the kingdom of God. It is the community that builds up; it is the community which helps sustain; and it is the community that also holds each member accountable in love. Sometimes, faith communities have forgotten their own mission.

While the disciples were forming these faith communities in Jerusalem and Judea, a man from Tarsus was having his own encounter with the resurrected Christ. Saul of Tarsus had a multi-layered experience with the resurrected Christ that turned his world upside down. Saul, now named Paul, had been the most zealous persecutor of Christians. After his encounter with the resurrected Christ, he not only became a believer in Jesus, but he became the most zealous proclaimer of the gospel message. Paul's personal mission was to carry the gospel message to the non-Jews, to the Gentiles. He was sharing his God story everywhere he went in the known Roman world proclaiming Christ as Lord. Paul is an example of how to overcome culture to win souls for Christ. Paul was a visionary leader and demonstrates for us how we as the church are to be the instrument, the sign, and the foretaste of what is to come.[106] Paul would not deviate from his God given mission. Paul was moving out of his comfort zone into unknown territories to form new faith communities.

Paul went on three missionary journeys to plant new churches in the Roman world. Some call his final trip to Rome, when he was bound in chains, his fourth missionary journey as he never stopped proclaiming the gospel of Jesus, even when he was a state prisoner. Paul had a pattern for sharing his God story. He would usually have a partner in ministry whom he was training. This missionary team

103 Romans 8:11, NRSV.
104 Dr. Kendall Soulen, Systematic Lecture Notes 3/9/06.
105 The Book of Discipline of the United Methodist Church, paragraph 120.
106 J. R. Woodward, *Creating a Missional Culture: Equipping the Church for the Sake of the World.* (Westmont, IL, IVP books, 2012), p. 28.

would arrive in a new city and they would begin their proclamation in the synagogue, since Paul himself was a Pharisee. Paul would begin his God story with the history of the Jews. He would then introduce Jesus as the Messiah for whom the Israelites had been waiting. Then Paul would speak of his own personal life encounter with Jesus of Nazareth and how Paul himself was a new creation because of Jesus. While there are variations on this methodology, this was the primary way in which Paul would plant a new church.

Paul's speech usually divided the listeners into three groups: Some would want to hear more; some would want to be baptized immediately; and some called Paul blasphemous and they tried to throw him out of the city. At that point tension filled the air: Paul would begin a house church in the city, this would become the church plant, and those who thought Paul was being unfaithful to the God of Israel would begin to plot against him.

Paul met adversity every step of the way. Yet, the adversity did not stop him from sharing the gospel message. In his own words these are some of the trials he faced in sharing his God stories. "I have been in prison more frequently, been flogged more severely, and been exposed to death again and again. Five times I received from the Jews the forty lashes minus one. Three times I was beaten with rods, once I was pelted with stones, three times I was shipwrecked, I spent a night and a day in the open sea, I have been constantly on the move. I have been in danger from rivers, in danger from bandits, in danger from my fellow Jews, in danger from Gentiles; in danger in the city, in danger in the country, in danger at sea; and in danger from false believers. I have labored and toiled and have often gone without sleep; I have known hunger and thirst and have often gone without food; I have been cold and naked."[107]

These are some of the adversities Paul faced. What adversities are we willing to face in order to share the gospel message? What are we willing to do to move God's plan forward, knowing we were created for a purpose, knowing that our story is part of God's greater story? Our current culture is moving farther and farther away from being a Christian culture. In that future, we will be facing more and more adversity in sharing our God stories. What are we willing to do to advance the plot of God's story for the kingdom of God? Are we, like Paul, "Willing to become all things to all people so that some might be saved?"[108]

Paul was willing to advance the plot by meeting the culture where they were and by sharing his God stories. Perhaps the most famous example of Paul meeting local culture was when he arrived in Athens. In observing the city, he was greatly disturbed by all of the pagan statues to various gods that he found. Paul was invited before the Areopagus, which was a type of judicial council located on Mars Hill, a bare marble hill next to the Acropolis. This was the place where the Areopagus met, and learned minds discussed the latest philosophies. Paul began his speech by praising the Athenians for having a desire to be "religious," and then Paul connected their religiosity to Jesus by proclaiming the identity of the "altar to the unknown god." Paul proclaims to them, "The God who made the world and everything in it is the Lord of heaven and earth and does not live in temples built by human hands. And he is not served by human hands, as if he needed anything. Rather, he himself gives everyone life and breath and everything else."[109] Paul continues to proclaim why God desires relationship with humans. "God did this

---

107 2 Corinthians 11:23-27, NIV.
108 1 Corinthians 9:22, NIV.
109 Acts 17:24-25, NIV.

so that they [humans] would seek him and perhaps reach out for him and find him, though he is not far from any one of us."[110]

We often wonder what drove Paul to risk everything in order to tell his God stories. Sometimes we may wonder what the driving force is for us to tell our God stories. We have biblical mandates, from the Great Commission in Matthew 28 to Jesus telling us that we are a sent people. In addition, in every speech in the book of Acts, every speech that proclaims what God has done, there is the Greek word *Dei* that is often translated as, "It is necessary." This word is understood as the divine authority for "it is necessary." Theologian Soards tells us, "The speeches in Acts tell of a transcendent but active God who relates to the world, especially to humans, in order to bring to fruition God's own divine will. God intervenes in life in this world to initiate relationships, to give direction for present or future actions and to reverse the course of events by undoing certain effects which result from particular humanly initiated causes that are inconsistent with God's own purposes."[111]

The driving force behind Paul's work of planting churches and sharing his God stories is that it was divinely necessary for God's plan to be carried out. Paul was a part of that plan. Paul plainly states, "I do all this for the sake of the gospel, that I may share in its blessings."[112] We as modern day Christians are a part of that plan. Once again, "God's plan" is often brought forth in the speeches. The speeches in Acts bring forth the message that "God's plan" has now been and is being brought to realization. What is that plan? That God in the flesh, Jesus, would make a path for right relationship to bridge the divide between a holy God and sinful people. That God would be in right relationship with God's people, through accepting Jesus as our Lord and Savior, and that the new creation, the kingdom of God, would be ushered into the world.

Paul understood himself to be united with God as part of God's plan to advance the gospel. We, too, should understand ourselves to be part of God's divine plan to advance the kingdom of God "On earth as it is in heaven." Therefore, it is divinely necessary, *Dei*, for us to share our own God stories to advance the larger plot of God's story. What a privilege it is for us to share in the blessing of sharing the gospel message!

This is where we see the idea of the faith community and the gospel message moving forward hand in hand. "Christ wants to create 'a people,' not merely isolated individuals who believe in him."[113] Remember when we began this study we saw God creating a people for God's self through Abraham and his descendants. This community of faith has evolved and is now to be lived out in the life of the church. Church is not to be some isolated event that we attend on Sundays and then leave out of our lives for the remainder of the week. Rather, God wants us thinking about our relationship with God 24/7. The church community exists to be the hands and feet of Christ, empowered by the Holy Spirit. Scottish theologian and pastor, Sinclair Ferguson, says it like this, "We are not saved individually and then choose to join the church as if it were some club or support group. Christ died for all people, and we are saved when, by faith, we become part of the people for whom Christ died. The story of the Bible is the story of God fulfilling the promise, 'I will take you as my own people, and I will be your God.'[114] If the

---

110 Acts 17:27, NIV.

111 Marion L. Soardes, *The Speeches in Acts. Their Content, Context, and Concerns.* (Louisville, KY, Westminster Knox Press, 1994) p.184.

112 1 Corinthians 9:23, NIV.

113 Tim Chester and Steve Timmis, *Total Church. A Radical Reshaping around Gospel and Community.* (Wheaton, Il, Crossway Publishing, 2008) p.39.

114 Exodus 6:7, NIV.

gospel is to be at the heart of church life and mission, it is equally true that the church is to be at the heart of the gospel life and mission."[115]

Some of us might benefit from constructing a new vision for our lives that is centered on the gospel message and our faith community. Over the years the vision and mission of the church has become clouded and redefined by our culture. Instead of being central to our lives, we, over time, have constructed our own opinions over whether we need to be part of a faith community and whether we have a personal desire to share our God stories. It is so much easier to let someone else do that!

Here is the reality. God calls us each to be part of advancing the gospel message through sharing our God stories. Our God stories are more easily told when we are part of a faith community where we can be built up to go back out into the world and share the divine vision. It is divinely necessary that we all participate in God's vision. Sometimes it seems that churches have lost the vision and have become inwardly focused instead of outwardly focused. We have forgotten that we exist for God, rather than God existing for us. Theologian Douglas Powe hits the nail on the head with his statement that, "The need for a different vision often makes no sense to those who have constructed their lives around the old vision."[116] Is our vision of church and the sharing of our God stories constructed around our own personal ideas, or is it centered on the bigger story that fulfills God's purposes?

---

115 Tim Chester and Steve Timmis, p. 39.

116 Douglas F. Powe, Jr., *New Wine New Wineskins: How African American Congregations Can Reach New Generations.* (Nashville, TN, Abingdon Press, 2012), p. 39.

SMALL GROUP LEADER DISCUSSION - WEEK SIX

1. What is the purpose of the church and the inherent job of the faith community?

   a. What is the purpose of the universal church? Check out your denominational resources to see what they say about the church.

   b. What difference would it make if your church were not in your community? Would anyone miss it? Would the community around your church miss your church?

   c. How does a faith community: Continue to usher in the kingdom of God; Build up the community of faith; Sustain and nurture each other; Hold each member accountable in love?

2. When we face adversity in sharing our God stories, do we stop in our tracks because it is too hard, or do we move forward like Paul, knowing that we are advancing the plot of God's story?

3. Read the account of Paul's speech to the Areopagus in Acts 17:16-34.

   a. What words jump out at you in reading this speech?

   b. What cultural issues was Paul addressing in this speech?

   c. How could you form the sharing of your God story in a similar pattern to Paul's speech?

4. Is your personal life centered on both gospel and faith community?

   a. What would it take to be more centered in gospel and faith community?

   b. What changes or what mindsets would have to be different in order to live this out 24/7?

5. What characteristics show that Paul was a visionary leader?

6. The divine "It is necessary" is found in virtually every speech in the book of the Acts of the Apostles. How does this word *Dei* play a role in advancing the gospel message?

   a. How does this word and mandate inspire you to move out of your comfort zone to share your God story?

   b. In some translations, the word *Dei* is not translated at all, or it is translated as must, ought, or should. These translation decisions render the passages less effective. In order to see the full effect of this word you might like to do a Greek word search on the book of Acts. Try this site: www.blueletterbible.org. Search the word "necessary." Now click on the "tools" on the left and click "interlinear." See the word *Dei*, now click on Strong's number G 1163. Observe that this word is used over 103 times in the New Testament, of which 22 are in Acts.

DAILY DEVOTIONALS - WEEK SIX

SHARING YOUR STORY - MOVING BEYOND COMFORT ZONES

DAY 1 **SHARED FAITH. KNOCK - KNOCK. WHO'S THERE?** **LUKE 11:9**

"So I say to you, 'Ask, and it will be given you; search, and you will find; knock, and the door will be opened for you. For everyone who asks receives, and everyone who searches finds, and for everyone who knocks, the door will be opened.'" NRSV

Knock—knock.
Who's there?
Luke.
Luke who?
Luke through the peep hole and find out.[117]

Knock—knock jokes are a familiar part of childhood. Just say the words "Knock—knock" and we automatically know what we are supposed to say next, "Who's there?" The thing that makes knock—knock jokes work is not the "punny" punch line. It's the "Who's there?" Without someone to ask the question "Who's there?" there is no joke.

As a shy, overweight, and awkward child, I was obsessed with knock-knock jokes. It was the one way I was sure that people were listening. So when I prayed I would begin, "Knock—knock, God." In my young heart I knew God was listening because I said, "Knock—knock, God," and I imagined God answering, "Who's there?" As an adult my prayers have changed, however, there are still times I say, "Knock—knock, God." Whenever I feel that my prayers are only making it to the ceiling, or I need assurance that God is listening, I begin my prayer, "Knock—knock, God." Instead of imagining God answering, "Who's there?" I imagine God saying, "Come in."

Jesus said in Luke 11:9 that if we knock the door will be opened. When we pray we can have assurance that God is listening and invites us in.

Reflection: Have there been times when you felt that God did not hear your prayers? What did you do? How do you experience God hearing your prayers? Is there a story here that you can share with someone else who might have had that same experience?

Prayer: Knock—knock, God. I know you are listening and that you invite me in. Help me to search for you and hear you when you say, "Come in." Amen. -Rev. Sherri Comer-Cox

Notes:

---

117 http://www.funology.com

DAILY DEVOTIONALS - WEEK SIX

SHARING YOUR STORY - MOVING BEYOND COMFORT ZONES

DAY 2   **WRESTLE WITH THE WORD.**   **2 TIMOTHY 3:16-17**

"All Scripture is inspired by God and is useful for teaching, for reproof, for correction, and for training in righteousness, so that everyone who belongs to God may be proficient, equipped for every good work." NRSV

As a seminary student I was challenged to "sift through Scripture." Until going to seminary I thought I was supposed to read my Bible but not fret about the parts that were confusing to me. However, in seminary I had to wrestle with Scripture I did not understand. In wrestling with the Word I learned to read Scripture in context of who the first readers of Scripture were and through the lens of their cultural, economic, and geographical background. It was challenging, but prepared me as a pastor and a disciple of Christ. In 2 Timothy, Paul tells us that all Scripture is inspired by God and useful for us. Even the parts we find confusing or challenging. The amazing thing about the Bible is that it is useful for every person in every country in whatever situation they are experiencing. Most of us have bought books that tell us how to diet, to invest our money, or succeed at something. I confess I have a stack of "How To Books" somewhere in my house. Although I own these books, they are useless unless I actually read them. Just like owning a diet book does not make a person skinny, owning a Bible does not equip us for every good work. We have to actually read, sift through, and wrestle with the Word because it is "useful for teaching, for reproof, for correction, and for training in righteousness."

Reflection: What is the biggest challenge for you in reading the Bible? What can you do to overcome it? What would you say to someone who says, "I don't understand the Bible and when I read it I don't get anything out of it?"

Prayer: God of Word and Wonder, thank you for speaking to me through Scripture. Help me with the Scripture I find challenging and open my ears to hear you when I read and meditate on your Holy Word. Amen. -Rev. Sherri Comer-Cox

Notes:

SHARING YOUR STORY - MOVING BEYOND COMFORT ZONES

DAY 3 WHERE HAVE YOU SEEN GOD? 1 CORINTHIANS 12:4-11

"Now there are varieties of gifts, but the same Spirit; and there are varieties of services, but the same Lord; and there are varieties of activities, but it is the same God who activates all of them in everyone. To each is given the manifestation of the Spirit for the common good. To one is given through the Spirit the utterance of wisdom, and to another the utterance of knowledge according to the same Spirit, to another faith by the same Spirit, to another gifts of healing by the one Spirit, to another the working of miracles, to another prophecy, to another the discernment of spirits, to another various kinds of tongues, to another the interpretation of tongues. All these are activated by one and the same Spirit, who allots to each one individually just as the Spirit chooses." NRSV

As someone who loves to preach, I sometimes forget that there are those who have a fear of public speaking. So, when we began having a time of praise and testimony in our worship service I was disappointed that more people did not speak up when asked the question, "Where have you seen God in your life this week?" I was thrilled that some people would share their praise and joys but still felt a sense of frustration that more people did not share. When I shared my frustrations with a member of the worship team she set me straight. She asked me if I liked to cook. I answered with a swift and loud, "No!" "Why not?" she asked. I explained that cooking was a chore for me and I dreaded planning daily meals, grocery shopping, and cooking...I would rather... "Give a speech?" she asked. She then reminded me that some of the folks who did not speak up during the praise and testimony time of worship are the same folks who serve the church and Kingdom of God in humility and grace. Point taken.

God gives all of us gifts, talents, and strengths. Some people can share their testimony and joys with their voices. Others answer the question, "Where have you seen God?" through their service to others. The important thing to remember is it is the same Spirit, the same Lord, who receives the praise!

Reflection: What gifts and talents do you have that help you answer the question "Where have you seen God?"

Prayer: Lord God, thank you for gifting me with everything I need to see you in my life. Help me to use the gifts that you have given me so that others might see you through me. I give you all the praise and glory for my life! In Christ's name, Amen. -Rev. Sherri Comer-Cox

Notes:

DAILY DEVOTIONALS - WEEK SIX

SHARING YOUR STORY - MOVING BEYOND COMFORT ZONES

DAY 4   **I'M JUST SAYIN'.**   **1 PETER 4:11**

"If anyone speaks, he should do it as one speaking the very words of God. If anyone serves, he should do it with the strength God provides, so that in all things God may be praised through Jesus Christ. To him be the glory and the power for ever and ever. Amen." NRSV

There is a popular phrase that I hear or say oodles of times a day. I bet you have heard it or even said it, too. "I'm just sayin'." It's a funny little phrase that we use at the end of some sort of declaration. Sort of like, "That's the way I see it, I'm just sayin'." I started thinking about that pithy phrase a few days ago. It is easy to *just say*, but it is the *doing* that is a little more challenging. There is another phrase that I have heard, "All talk, no walk."

In today's Scripture passage, Peter lumps all the spiritual gifts into two categories: speaking *and* serving. These gifts are not to be used separately but together so people will know Jesus, and God will be glorified. In God's infinite wisdom, God gifted some to speak and some to serve. What would the church look like if it was "all talk"? Whether we are speaking for God or serving God, the important thing to remember is that even though we provide the willingness to speak or serve, it is God who provides the strength. Peter also tells us that when we speak and serve, it should be for God's glory, not ours. I'm just sayin'.

Reflection: Do you feel more comfortable speaking or serving? If you are more comfortable speaking, how can you use it in unison with serving? If you are more comfortable with serving, how can you use it in unison with speaking? Examining where we lead best can empower us to share our stories in new ways.

Prayer: Lord, thank you for a voice to speak and hands and feet to serve and I pray that you give me opportunities to glorify you. May everything I say and everything I do praise you! In the name of Jesus the Christ, Amen. -Rev. Sherri Comer-Cox

Notes:

SHARING YOUR STORY - MOVING BEYOND COMFORT ZONES

DAY 5   **SELECTIVE HEARING.**   **ROMANS 10:14-18**

"But how are they to call on one in whom they have not believed? And how are they to believe in one of whom they have never heard? And how are they to hear without someone to proclaim him? And how are they to proclaim him unless they are sent? As it is written, 'How beautiful are the feet of those who bring good news!' But not all have obeyed the good news; for Isaiah says, 'Lord, who has believed our message?' So faith comes from what is heard, and what is heard comes through the word of Christ. But I ask, have they not heard? Indeed they have; for 'Their voice has gone out to all the earth and their words to the ends of the world.'" NRSV

A few years ago my husband and I noticed that we were having a communication problem. We were always saying, "You didn't say that" or "You didn't ask me to do that." After a few weeks of this we realized that it was not what was being said, but what was being heard. This is a common condition in marriages that you may have also experienced; Selective Hearing. It can be extremely frustrating to tell someone something and realize that they have not heard a word you said. A friend of mine deals with this condition by beginning every important conversation with the word "football" because she knows that will get her husband's attention. How many of us as youngsters acted like we did not hear our parents calling us because we wanted to avoid a punishment or some chore?

Sometimes this is our response to God. We hear only what we want to hear. Jesus used the phrase, "If anyone has ears to hear, let them hear"[118] eight times in Scripture to get people's attention. We use selective hearing with God because we do not want to do what God's Word tells us to do. After all, God's Word may tell us to change the way we are doing something, forgive someone we don't think should be forgiven, or go somewhere we don't want to go. Selective hearing is a chancy thing when it comes to hearing God's voice. If we are not listening to God's voice when God asks us to do something difficult, we may not hear God speak love and grace to us, either. What would it look like when we pray to keep our hearts and ears tuned in to what God may say? Faith comes from hearing. As we listen for God's voice in our lives, we should be ready to do what God calls us to do, even if it means speaking love and grace to someone who has selective hearing.

Reflection: Do you think you have selective hearing with God? Has there been a time that you felt God telling you do something uncomfortable (such as sharing your testimony, feeding the hungry, or giving to the poor) and you ignored God? What was the source of your selective hearing?

Prayer: God, there are times I want to hear you and times I ignore you when you call. Please help me to listen with my heart and my ears when you speak, and give me the strength to do what you say. Amen.
-Rev. Sherri Comer-Cox

Notes:

---

118 Mark 4:23, NIV.

DAILY DEVOTIONALS - WEEK SIX

SHARING YOUR STORY - MOVING BEYOND COMFORT ZONES

DAY 6   **THE GOLDEN RULE.**   **MATTHEW 7:12**

"In everything do to others as you would have them do to you." NRSV

This little Bible verse, the Golden Rule, is one of the most quoted verses in the Bible. It's a simple concept; treat others the way you want to be treated. Many of us try to keep the Golden Rule, but at times it is difficult. If you have ever driven on the beltway into Washington D.C. during rush hour, you know what I mean! We think of the Golden Rule as a way of showing kindness to our fellow human beings. But is that all there is to it? A dear friend showed me another way to live the Golden Rule as a follower of Christ. "What is the best thing anyone has ever done for you?" she asked. "The best thing anyone ever did for me was to tell me about Jesus," I answered. I continued, "It's the best thing Christians can do for others." "Then as disciples of Christ who obey the Golden Rule and do to others as we would have them do to us, why aren't more Christians sharing the Good News?" Her understanding of the Golden Rule humbled me.

If you have experienced God's forgiveness and saving grace, you understand what an amazing gift it is. I am so grateful to the woman who cared enough to share the Good News of Jesus Christ with me. As Christians obeying and living the Golden Rule, we have a motivation to share the Good News with others. One of the best things we can do to others, as we would have them do to us, is share the saving grace of Jesus Christ and proclaim the Good News!

Reflection: Who told you about Jesus? How are you going to live the Golden Rule and "In everything do to others as you would have them do unto you?"

Prayer: God, sometimes it is difficult to treat others the way I want to be treated. Help me live the Golden Rule and tell others about Jesus, just as someone shared the Good News with me. In Christ Jesus, Amen. -Rev. Sherri Comer-Cox

Notes:

DAILY DEVOTIONALS - WEEK SIX

SHARING YOUR STORY - MOVING BEYOND COMFORT ZONES

DAY 7　　　　　　　**ALL THINGS TO ALL PEOPLE.**　　　　　**1 CORINTHIANS 9:19-23**

"For though I am free with respect to all, I have made myself a slave to all, so that I might win more of them. To the Jews I became as a Jew, in order to win Jews. To those under the law I became as one under the law (though I myself am not under the law) so that I might win those under the law. To those outside the law I became as one outside the law (though I am not free from God's law but am under Christ's law) so that I might win those outside the law. To the weak I became weak, so that I might win the weak. I have become all things to all people; that I might by all means save some. I do it all for the sake of the gospel, so that I may share in its blessings." NRSV

In my life before becoming a United Methodist pastor, I was a preschool teacher and I loved teaching the children in my care. One of the main things I learned as a preschool teacher is that I had to speak on their level. Most of the time that meant getting on my knees so I could also be on their eye level. My voice and language changed when I spoke to the children. I adapted myself to the children's world. I used words like "doggie" or "poopie." I also learned about the things that the children liked. To this day I can still sing most of the Barney and Sesame Street songs! Using child-like words and learning to sing silly songs did not change who I was, but it did help me identify with the children and it helped them to trust me.

I think this is what Paul was telling us in today's Scripture. When witnessing, Paul adapted himself to the situation in order to share the gospel in a way that could be understood by those listening to the message. Paul crossed cultural, religious, political, and economic barriers to share the Good News of Jesus Christ. Although Paul was flexible in his methods, he never compromised his faith. When we share the Good News of Christ we must remember the lesson from Paul. The way we present the message may change in order to speak to a particular group of people, but the message does not change. In order to reach every person everywhere, we need to learn how to become all things to all people without compromising the message so that people will be saved. As we do this for the sake of the gospel, we will share in the blessings of God's grace!

Reflection: How do you identify with people who are different than you? What can you do to help you identify with others for the sake of sharing the Good News of Christ?

Prayer: Lord, thank you for your saving work on the cross. When Paul walked the earth, he became all things to all people in order that "some might be saved" by sharing the good news of Jesus.[119] Help me to be like Paul so I can be all things to all people in order to save some. In Christ's name. Amen. -Rev. Sherri Comer-Cox

Notes:

---

119 1 Corinthians 9:22, NIV.

SERMON OUTLINE - WEEK SIX

SHARING YOUR STORY - MOVING BEYOND COMFORT ZONES

1 Corinthians 9:19-23; Acts 17:16-34

1. Parents, help me fill in the blank.

    a. Your kids are complaining about doing something that you asked them to do.

    b. You do your best to explain the entire reason of why they need to obey.

    c. Finally, out of frustration, when your child asks you one more time, "Why?"

        i. What does your answer become?

        ii. "Why?" "Because I said so."

2. Now, if we want to dig deeper into that phrase, as I have often done with my children, it becomes something like this.

    a. God entrusted you to me while you grow up.

    b. It is my job to make sure that you are safe, protected, and learn to be independent.

    c. In addition, it is my responsibility to help you grow up knowing Jesus and knowing how Jesus would want you to act.

    d. This is my responsibility to God, to raise you well.

3. Just as God has entrusted the next generation to us through our offspring, so too, God has entrusted the church to us.

    a. The very nature of the church is to be the vehicle through which disciples are made.

    b. Just like the family unit is to be the vehicle through which we raise our children.

    c. The church is the community in which that family is to be nurtured in Christ.

        i. We teach about Jesus.

        ii. We teach about who God is and how God acts in the world.

        iii. We continue this process through confirmation.

        iv. We continue this process every week through Sunday School, and we are so grateful for our Sunday School teachers!

        v. We continue this process through our Vacation Bible Camp, and if you are not signed up for VBC, please do so, it is a great way to serve and a great way to nurture our children.

4. We are in week six of a seven week series on sharing your God story.

    a. Last week we learned that it is the job of the church to nurture each other and tell the story.

    b. The church was birthed for the purpose of continuing what God (in human form, Jesus) began on earth.

    c. Sometimes we are like kids and we want to say "Why?"

    d. Why do I have to tell the story, can't that be someone else's job?

    e. I am sure that is only the job of the pastor, but not me, I am an ordinary person.

  f. Why?... just like the kids...

  g. And do you want to know God's answer...?

    i. It is as good as our answers as parents...

    ii. We have shown the texts that tell us to go make disciples, and that Jesus says as the father has sent me..., yet, sometimes we still ask why.

    iii. The answer is...We have seen that from the beginning of the biblical witness, we were created as God's people to be a blessing for others.

    iv. The other reason we are to tell our God stories...

    v. Wait for it...is

    vi. Because "God said so." Really.

5. *Dei*

  a. Little Greek word that means, "it was necessary."

  b. This word is used often in the book of Acts. *Dei.*

  c. And it means "the Divine necessary," it was necessary, is the divine encounter

  d. Think about it, this is really saying, "Because I said so."

  e. It was necessary...

    i. Sometimes the translation comes across as "you ought" or "you should," but the power behind this word is lost, because it is a divine act of ought or should.

    ii. The divine, "It was necessary."

6. We might be asking, well God, fine, but what was necessary?

  a. The Divine plan, this is also often referred to in the book of Acts.

  b. This is the divine plan that we share in telling God's story!

  c. The entire book of Acts tells about this divine plan of empowering disciples to move out of their comfort zones for something bigger, something more important.

    i. First the disciples, now turned apostles, moving out of their comfort zones to share the good news.

    ii. Performing miracles, just like Jesus, to show they were living in the power of the Holy Spirit, just as Jesus was doing.

    iii. Then Paul, Christian killer, now turned biggest proclaimer of Jesus.

    iv. He has a divine encounter with the resurrected Jesus.

    v. Then Paul moves out of his comfort zone to share the story.

    vi. Not only does he move out of his comfort zone, he goes on three missionary trips to plant churches; to start new faith communities. Some would say his final trip to Rome in chains was his fourth missionary journey.

  d. WHY? Because this is the divine plan.

7. This is how Paul worked:

SERMON OUTLINE - WEEK SIX

   a.   Enter a city, start in the synagogue.

   b.   Begin with their common Jewish heritage.

   c.   Next tell of Jesus who is God in the flesh.

   d.   In each case, some would believe, and some would not.

     i.   Some would call him blasphemous and attempt to kick him out of the city.

     ii.   Some would get violent with him.

     iii.   He was beaten, stoned, shipwrecked, whipped.

        1.   And guess what? He continued to tell the story of God.

        2.   Nothing would stop him from moving forward with his God story.

        3.   This God who had given him new life.

     iv.   So we hear him say words like this:

"Though I am free and belong to no one, I have made myself a slave to everyone, to win as many as possible. To the Jews I became like a Jew, to win the Jews. To those under the law I became like one under the law (though I myself am not under the law), so as to win those under the law. To those not having the law I became like one not having the law (though I am not free from God's law but am under Christ's law), so as to win those not having the law. To the weak I became weak, to win the weak. I have become all things to all people so that by all possible means I might save some. I do all this for the sake of the gospel, that I may share in its blessings." (1 Corinthians 9:19 - 23 NIV)

8.   Why does he do this?

   a.   All this for the sake of the gospel, that he may share in its blessings.

   b.   This goes back to the "blessed to be a blessing" idea.

     i.   Remember where we began this study, with Abraham, and his descendants. We are blessed to be a blessing.

     ii.   We now see that Paul has continued that theme of sharing God's story throughout the biblical witness AND Paul now says the way he is blessed is by sharing the story.

     iii.   He is blessed when he can share the gospel message.

     iv.   He is blessed when he can share his God story that intersects with his own life story.

     v.   He is blessed when he is persecuted for the sake of Jesus Christ.

9.   Really? Blessed when he is persecuted?

   a.   Is that even on our radars?

   b.   It is not even in our thought process.

   c.   Blessed when we are persecuted for the sake of sharing the gospel of Jesus.

   d.   Paul was often persecuted when he shared his witness about Jesus.

     i.   Stoned, shipwrecked, put in prison, you name it...

    ii. All because he was following God's divine plan.

        1. Yet he never said, "enough God, it is time for me to retire."

        2. He never said, "this is too hard"...he kept going.

        3. He was always discerning God's next step for his life.

        4. Always discerning the next place God wanted him to go.

        5. And always connecting to the people beginning with where they were in their culture.

10. Listen to an example of how Paul connected with the local people, people he did not know, people he had just met; people with whom he wanted to share his God story.

    a. This is in the middle of his second missionary journey in Athens.

"While Paul was waiting for them in Athens, he was greatly distressed to see that the city was full of idols. So he reasoned in the synagogue with both Jews and God-fearing Greeks, as well as in the marketplace day by day with those who happened to be there. A group of Epicurean and Stoic philosophers began to debate with him. Some of them asked, "What is this babbler trying to say?" Others remarked, "He seems to be advocating foreign gods." They said this because Paul was preaching the good news about Jesus and the resurrection. Then they took him and brought him to a meeting of the Areopagus, where they said to him, 'May we know what this new teaching is that you are presenting? You are bringing some strange ideas to our ears, and we would like to know what they mean.' (All the Athenians and the foreigners who lived there spent their time doing nothing but talking about and listening to the latest ideas.)

Paul then stood up in the meeting of the Areopagus and said: 'People of Athens! I see that in every way you are very religious. For as I walked around and looked carefully at your objects of worship, I even found an altar with this inscription: TO AN UNKNOWN GOD. *So you are ignorant of the very thing you worship—and this is what I am going to proclaim to you.'*

'The God who made the world and everything in it is the Lord of heaven and earth and does not live in temples built by human hands. And he is not served by human hands, as if he needed anything. Rather, he himself gives everyone life and breath and everything else. From one man he made all the nations, that they should inhabit the whole earth; and he marked out their appointed times in history and the boundaries of their lands. God did this so that they would seek him and perhaps reach out for him and find him, though he is not far from any one of us. For in him we live and move and have our being.' As some of your own poets have said, 'We are his offspring.'

'Therefore since we are God's offspring, we should not think that the divine being is like gold or silver or stone—an image made by human design and skill. In the past God overlooked such ignorance, but now he commands all people everywhere to repent. For he has set a day when he will judge the world with justice by the man he has appointed. He has given proof of this to everyone by raising him from the dead.'

When they heard about the resurrection of the dead, some of them sneered, but others said, 'We want to hear you again on this subject.' At that, Paul left the Council. Some of the people became followers of Paul and believed. Among them was Dionysius, a member of the Areopagus, also a woman named Damaris, and a number of others." (Acts 17: 16 - 33 NIV)

    b. Paul connected the culture with the gospel message

        i. He connected their "religiosity" to Jesus.

        ii. Friends, we can connect our culture to God as well.

SERMON OUTLINE - WEEK SIX

       iii. It is part of our mandate, it is part of our job as Christians... and,

       iv. "It is divinely necessary."

11. Why is it divinely necessary?

    a. Because the gospel, the good news of Jesus' life, death, and resurrection goes hand in hand with community.

    b. Gospel and community together.

    c. He could have just had individuals accept Christ and be done with them, but that was not Paul's understanding of what God wanted him to do.

    d. He was called to form community, God's community.

       i. The church is the best way we have to live out the life message of Jesus.

       ii. The best way we have to live out the gospel and to share the gospel.

12. Maybe you have heard someone say, "I believe in Jesus, but I don't believe in organized religion."

    a. That is unbiblical.

    b. Why? Because the church was God's idea, it was not the idea of humans.

    c. The problem is that the life of the church is lived out by humans who are fallible and sinful people.

    d. We do the best we can in being who God called us to be.

       i. We do the best we can at living out the message.

       ii. We share our story and live it out.

13. Paul moved out of his comfort zone to share the good news of Jesus and to form new communities in Christ—to plant churches.

    a. We, too, are called to move out of our comfort zones to share the story of Jesus, to share how our stories have intersected with that of Jesus.

    b. We do this so that others might come into a saving relationship with Jesus.

    c. Here is the main idea. It is divinely necessary to further God's bigger plan of redemption for all of creation, because God has mandated it as so.

    d. You and I have a job to do.

       i. Sometimes it means moving out of our comfort zones...

       ii. Are you willing to live into it?

       iii. Are you willing to live into the purpose for what God created you to do and be?

Amen.

LITURGY FOR WORSHIP - WEEK SIX

SHARING YOUR STORY - MOVING BEYOND COMFORT ZONES

FIRST SCRIPTURE READING: 1 CORINTHIANS 9:19-23

READING BEFORE THE SERMON: ACTS 17:16-34

CALL TO WORSHIP: (Based on Acts 17)
God who made the world and everything in it, we gather to worship you.
For it is in you that we live and move and have our being.
Shake down our world of idols, so that we might stay focused on you.
For it is in you that we live and move and have our being.
We praise you for our "appointed time in history," and give thanks for the unique way you designed each of us.
For it is in you that we live and move and have our being.
In this gathering place, give us repentant hearts, so that we might serve you with all of our being.
For it is in you that we live and move and have our being.
May our worship and praise this morning be pleasing to you, for it is in you that we live and move and have our being.

PRAYER OF CONFESSION: (Based on 1 Corinthians 9)
God of All Created Beings, Becoming all things to all people is not easy. While you have a special love for each of your created persons, we sometimes struggle to love as you love. We sometimes struggle to have the desire to be all things to all people, so that they might come into a saving relationship with you. God, change our hearts. Shape us and mold us into your image, so that we can love as you love, so that we can serve as you call us to serve, and so that by our stories, actions, and deeds, others might come to know you. Empower us by your Holy Spirit, in the name of Jesus. Amen.

POSSIBLE HYMNS:
2236   Gather Us In
2013   Bless the Lord My Soul
583   You Are the Seed
585   This Little Light of Mine

* *Three digit page numbers refer to the United Methodist Hymnal*
* *Four digit page numbers refer to The Faith We Sing Hymnal*

SPECIAL SONGS:
Go Light Your World by Kathy Troccoli

POSSIBLE PRAISE SONGS:
Your Grace is Enough by Chris Tomlin
He Reigns by Newsboys
Go by Newsboys
The Stand by Hillsong United
Because He Lives by Matt Maher
Forever Reign by Hillsong United
Grace so Glorious by Elevation Worship
Oceans by Hillsong United
I Am Not Alone by Kari Jobe
I Will Follow by Chris Tomlin

Week Seven
Life Intersections

What is your story?

SMALL GROUP LEADER - WEEK SEVEN

SHARING YOUR STORY - LIFE INTERSECTIONS

As we share our God stories, we will begin to notice patterns of God's grace. We increasingly become aware of these patterns during our own life transitions. In turn, we begin to see how our lives intersect with the multiple dimensions of God's story. As we grow more comfortable in sharing our God stories we begin to notice that we, too, grow relationally with the, "One in whom we live and move and have our being."[120] As we grow with the idea of being a blessing to others we begin to live the God story that we want to tell.

When we move beyond our comfort zones to share our God stories, two very important things happen within us: The first is that in the process of sharing our God stories, we become vulnerable. We become vulnerable and humble, just as God became vulnerable in becoming flesh. A vulnerable heart is a malleable heart. God can use us in a powerful way when our hearts are in-tune with God's heart. In short, we become more useful to God. In the process, we begin to, as Paul says, "Take captive every thought to make it obedient to Christ."[121]

Secondly, when we seek to know what our God story is and tell our God stories beyond our comfort zones, this process helps us grow ever deeper in our own relationship with God. Here is the reality. God does not *need* us. God can tell God's own story, but God *wants* us—God *desires* us. Why does God want us? This goes back to point one, God wants and desires our hearts. When we seek and desire to know God, we are growing in our relationship with our savior. That is exactly where God wants us. As we become more equipped to tell our stories, just by the process of becoming willing servants, we then begin to know who we are in Christ Jesus. We begin to claim the identity God intended for us. We might also begin to sense a purpose for our lives in the present here and now. As we become more closely identified with Jesus, through the sharing of our God stories, then we begin to operate out of the essential element of our lives, that of being a child of God.

Knowing our God stories helps empower us on our own faith journeys. Stories are often about the journey, not only the end product. This is the difference between caring if we alone are "saved" or caring enough to bring others with us on the journey. The stories of our journeys intersect with the journeys of other travelers and then our stories become intertwined, just as God's story is intertwined with our own story. As our journeys unfold, we begin to see these patterns of grace working in and through our God stories.

John Wesley, the unintentional founder of Methodism, experienced a heart that was strangely warmed. How did this happen? It did not happen from studies, but through real people sharing God stories— sharing faith journeys with him. In the fullness of time, an unwilling John Wesley had a God experience that was to change him and literally bring revival to England. Here is his description from his own diary of May 24, 1738: "In the evening I went very unwillingly to a society in Aldersgate Street, where one was reading Luther's preface to the Epistle to the Romans. About a quarter before nine, while he was describing the change which God works in the heart through faith in Christ, I felt my heart strangely warmed. I felt I did trust in Christ, Christ alone, for salvation; and an assurance was given me that He had taken away my sins, even mine, and saved me from the law of sin and death."[122]

---

120 Acts 17:28, NIV.
121 2 Corinthians 10:5, NIV.
122 John Wesley's diary, http://www.ccel.org/ccel/wesley/journal.vi.ii.xvi.html, accessed May 14, 2015.

Wesley had a conversion of the heart because someone was willing to share their faith story with him. He began to live the story that he wanted to tell. We can see throughout history that great leaders of the faith came to believe in Jesus because someone shared a God story with them. When we become willing servants, it allows us a deeper study of our own lives, and we discover that we, too, grow closer to our creator.

As we grow deeper in our own willingness to share our God stories, we will begin to notice these patterns of grace. After Wesley's conversion of the heart he began to map out the way God's grace works in our lives. Wesley believed that it is by God's grace that humans can be restored to the image of God. The image of God in which we were each made was lost when Sin entered the world. Each person was created in God's image, and that image of God in each individual needs to be restored. Wesley believed that the image of God can be restored in each of us—by grace. God's grace is offered to the life of a person in different ways by the power of the Holy Spirit, depending upon where that person is in their faith journey. Grace is a free gift offered wholly and without strings attached by a loving God who wants to bring all of creation back into relationship with God's self.

Wesley believed that prevenient grace is the way the Holy Spirit acts in the lives of people before they are even aware of God's presence in their lives. He believed that some type of intervention in the person's life awakens them to the presence of God and their own sinful nature. This intervention can be through hearing someone sharing their God story. Although God makes the first move towards redemption, each individual person must make the next step. It is up to each individual to accept that free grace from God. For Wesley, preaching and sharing of the good news through God stories is designed to awaken the soul of the listener to make them aware of their sinful nature, and to help them see the activity of the Holy Spirit that is already present in their lives through prevenient grace.

This pattern of grace continues in the next step which is called justification. Once again, God stories shared is a way for justification to be realized in a person's life. Justification defined is that by grace alone, in faith in Christ's saving work and not from any merit of our own, we are accepted by God and receive the Holy Spirit. The Holy Spirit renews our hearts while equipping and calling us to good works.[123] Justification is the work of the triune God. We are justified not through our own merits, but through the saving work of Jesus Christ who exchanges our cloak of sin for his cloak of righteousness. Once again, this pattern of grace becomes evident when we realize that our life stories are intersecting with God's bigger plan of redemption for the world.

So how did this justification take place in the first place? How did God show that love for each and every person? It was through the greater story of the saving work of Jesus Christ. It is only by the gift of what God has done through his Son Jesus Christ. Salvation from sin, and restoration to the image of God, or restored relationship with God, is only achieved through the saving work of Jesus Christ. This is God's overall story and is God's response to evil. God's story shared the gift of redemption through the saving power of Jesus Christ. At the cross, every power of evil, every power that could have severed love and destroyed relationships, was sent against Jesus. Yet the power of love between God the Father and the Son was stronger than any power that took Jesus to the cross. Jesus' love remained even towards those who nailed him to the cross. It showed that self-giving love is greater than any power of evil.[124]

123 Lutheran World Federation and The Roman Catholic Church, *The Joint Declaration on the Doctrine of Justification.* (Grand Rapids, Michigan, William B. Eerdman's Publishing Company, 1999), p.18.

124 Kendall Soulen, Systematic Lecture Notes 11/17/05.

SMALL GROUP LEADER - WEEK SEVEN

For Wesley, the patterns of grace and life intersections continue with the new birth or actual regeneration.[125] The Holy Spirit as giver of life is associated with this new birth for Christians. One way of talking about the experience of salvation or "being born anew" is regeneration or rebirth as a child of God. Just as the process of gestation in the womb takes place before we are born, so the process of being born again and becoming aware of the work of God is unfolding even now in our conscious lives. This process of being born anew is the work of the regeneration of the Holy Spirit; it takes time, yet we look forward to that new birth—being made complete in the future. This is the story of the new birth.

Our stories of grace can continue to be told through the process of assurance. Wesley believed that the faithful who are justified in Christ can rely on the promises of God. We were reminded in earlier chapters that God's promises do not come back empty. God *is* faithful. These promises are not only based on the character of God, but they are also based on the strengths of Jesus Christ's death and resurrection. The assurance of these promises can be built up in our own lives through receiving of the sacrament, such as communion, and listening to the Word. We can be assured of our salvation through the merits of the work of Jesus Christ. This assurance comes with the realization that we are justified before God by the faith we have in God.[126]

The final pattern of grace can be lived out by our faith stories in the process of sanctification. This is when we become willing servants of God, and this is when we begin to be willing to move out of our comfort zones to share our own stories of grace. The new birth is the initial step towards sanctification. Sanctification comes after we realize we are children of God, or after the new birth. This is a time we grow towards becoming more like the image of God. What does it mean to be made in the divine image of God? We can look to Jesus and see that answer. Sanctification is growing more like Jesus. We can grow more perfect in God's grace and more like Jesus by continuing to use the means of grace. The means of grace are practiced habits that bring us into right relationship with God such as: reading the Bible; weekly small group covenant practices; worship; receiving the Lord's Supper; prayer; and practicing acts of mercy. Using the means of grace is a continuing process for every Christian.

Sanctification is a real change. Sanctification is what God does *in us* through the Holy Spirit. It is what the Holy Spirit does in a believer's life to help them grow more and more in the image of God. It is being renewed by the Holy Spirit to be propelled into a new life as described in the new creation. It is the place where we see the results of the fruit of the Holy Spirit such as love, joy, peace, patience, kindness, goodness, faithfulness, gentleness and self-control.[127]

The means of grace given by Christ empower us to grow in grace.[128] Other means of grace include fasting, Christian conferencing, giving of our money, and ministry to the poor. Anything that would empower us to grow in holy living can be classified as a means of grace. This becomes a means of growing more like Jesus, closer to the image of God in which we were created. The means of grace are a way of conveying God's grace into the souls of humanity. Sharing our God stories also becomes a means of grace as we move closer into the sacred patterns established and mandated by God from the beginning of time. These patterns are to be lived out and shared with others, and they become a sacred means of grace.

---

125 John Wesley. *The Scripture Way of Salvation.* Wesley's Standard Sermons.
126 John Wesley. *Witness of the Spirit, Discourse II.* Wesley's Standard Sermons.
127 Galatians 5:22, NIV.
128 John Wesley. *The Means of Grace.* Wesley's Standard Sermons.

SMALL GROUP LEADER - WEEK SEVEN

Our life narrative embodies story telling of the sacred story in a form that can draw people into God's sacred narrative facilitating real transformation of lives. As we have seen in this study, our lives are created for the greater purpose of entering into the larger narrative story that is God's story for the universe. God chooses each of us to play a role in that narrative. We can choose to live into that call and bless the nations, or we can ignore the mandate. We can live the story we want to tell, or we can remain silent. Which will you choose?

SMALL GROUP LEADER DISCUSSION - WEEK SEVEN

1. This study has been all about sharing our God stories. This small group gives you an opportunity to articulate your story. You have a story that someone else needs to hear.

    a. How can you and your small group do a community project that would give you opportunities to share your God stories? This project could be a service project, an outreach project, or simply doing a prayer walk around the neighborhoods and praying that God will bring along the right opportunity to speak to someone, and that you will live into that opportunity.

    b. How can you "create" an opportunity to share a God story at work or at school or in line at the grocery store? Here is one example: You are in a restaurant. The server brings your food. You say, "Thank you. We are about to pray, would you like to join us or is there anything we can pray specifically for you?"[129]

2. Where is your life as defined by John Wesley's patterns of grace? (Have you experienced God's grace as prevenient, justified, or sanctified?)

    a. Do you use the means of grace regularly?

    b. What means of grace would you like to incorporate into your daily habits?

3. Have your ideas of why we share our God stories changed since the beginning of this study?

    a. What has changed for you?

    b. What concrete change will you make in sharing your God stories?

4. How have you grown relationally with God throughout this seven week study?

5. What would be the greatest benefit for YOU if you had a new opportunity to share your God story?

---

129 Original idea from Rev. William Chaney, Jr.

DAILY DEVOTIONALS - WEEK SEVEN

SHARING YOUR STORY - LIFE INTERSECTIONS

DAY 1   **BE ALERT - SET YOUR SPIRITUAL RADAR ON HIGH.**   LUKE 19:1-10

"Jesus entered Jericho and was passing through. A man was there by the name of Zacchaeus; he was a chief tax collector and was wealthy. He wanted to see who Jesus was, but because he was short he could not see over the crowd. So he ran ahead and climbed a sycamore-fig tree to see him, since Jesus was coming that way. When Jesus reached the spot, he looked up and said to him, 'Zacchaeus, come down immediately. I must stay at your house today.' So he came down at once and welcomed him gladly. All the people saw this and began to mutter, 'He has gone to be the guest of a sinner.' But Zacchaeus stood up and said to the Lord, 'Look, Lord! Here and now I give half of my possessions to the poor, and if I have cheated anybody out of anything, I will pay back four times the amount.' Jesus said to him, 'Today salvation has come to this house, because this man, too, is a son of Abraham. For the Son of Man came to seek and to save the lost.'" NIV

One hectic day, I rushed into the grocery store to run an errand. In the checkout line, my eyes fell on the word, "faith," tattooed on the young lady in front of me. After checking out, I hurried to my car and prepared to travel to my next appointment. Suddenly, I looked up and there she was—the tattooed young woman, carrying a heavy load of grocery bags, walking towards the street. I didn't have time; I didn't know her. But, I felt the pull of the Spirit and pulled up next to her, offering her a ride. "I was praying that someone would help me, and then you stopped," she said.

Jesus looked up and saw Zacchaeus. If anyone was overcommitted, bombarded by distractions, and preoccupied with deep thoughts, it was Jesus. Yet his spiritual radar was set on high, and Jesus saw this little man, hidden among the branches of the sycamore tree. Before we can share our stories, we have to be aware of those who need to hear.

Reflection: Is your spiritual radar on high? Who does God want you to invite to the banquet of God's love?

Prayer: Lord, open my eyes to see as you see. Move me from my own selfish agenda to really see the people you have placed in front of me who need your love. Amen. -Rev. Dana Werts

Notes:

DAILY DEVOTIONALS - WEEK SEVEN

SHARING YOUR STORY - LIFE INTERSECTIONS

DAY 2   **BE BOLD - TAKE A RELATIONAL RISK.**   **JOHN 4:7-10**

"When a Samaritan woman came to draw water, Jesus said to her, 'Will you give me a drink?' (His disciples had gone into the town to buy food.) The Samaritan woman said to him, 'You are a Jew and I am a Samaritan woman. How can you ask me for a drink?' (For Jews do not associate with Samaritans.) Jesus answered her, 'If you knew the gift of God and who it is that asks you for a drink, you would have asked him and he would have given you living water.'" NIV

I was preaching a sermon on homelessness, and wanted to interview a homeless person. At the church's soup kitchen, Larry and I discussed his experiences living under the bridge. This turned into a relationship that continued way beyond the sermon. We kept in touch through email, even after Larry moved away, and I was blessed to find out he now has a job and a home.

Larry shared with me that he longed for others to look at him as being human, instead of being seen as "vermin." It was a gift for someone to look him in the eye and smile, instead of avoiding him, afraid he might ask for a handout. Taking a risk relationally, I was deeply moved by how much God used Larry to teach and bless me, when I thought I would be the one helping Larry.

God took a relational risk, entering our world in Jesus Christ. God risked rejection, misunderstanding, and ridicule to reconcile the relationship between God and the people God created. Jesus reached out to the woman at the well to share "living water," taking a relational risk, especially in that culture. We cannot share our God stories, if we will not take relational risks. Maybe the first step is to really look others in the eye and smile, acknowledging their worth, even if they are different from us.

Reflection: Are you willing to risk a relationship with someone you don't know to love them as Christ loves us? What first step do you need to take to reach out?

Prayer: Lord, let our loving be bold. Let our actions and words reflect your bold love for us. Amen.
-Rev. Dana Werts

Notes:

SHARING YOUR STORY - LIFE INTERSECTIONS

DAY 3   **BE REAL - LET YOUR LIFE SONG SING.**   **2 CORINTHIANS 12:9-10**

"But he said to me, 'My grace is sufficient for you, for my power is made perfect in weakness.' Therefore I will boast all the more gladly about my weaknesses, so that Christ's power may rest on me. That is why, for Christ's sake, I delight in weaknesses, in insults, in hardships, in persecutions, in difficulties. For when I am weak, then I am strong." NIV

Some say that music is most powerful when it contains notes of dissonance, sounds that produce tension and a desire to be resolved. Concerned about what others think about us, we often want only our achievements and strengths to be the notes of our life song. However, it is those dissonant parts of our lives that sometimes speak most powerfully to others—the sin overcome, the fear removed, or the weakness that leads us to depend on God. Sharing honestly conveys that there is tension in the Christian life, places of weakness that we desire to be resolved, transformed. It is risky to be transparent to the world, but it is through honest testimony that God can speak with power to those who struggle with weakness and sin.

I struggle with Attention Deficit Syndrome. My desk reflects my struggle with organization. I finally confessed my need. Without judgment, a woman at church offered to organize my files. Her strength met my weakness and I was overwhelmed with thanksgiving and joy! God is able to harmonize our dissonant notes as we open our lives honestly to the love of God. This song of hope sings to the world, in need of healing and in need of joyous song.

Reflection: What are your dissonant notes or your areas of weakness? Does your life song proclaim to others the transforming power of God?

Prayer: Lord, I offer my life to you with all its conflicting notes and unresolved issues. Create a new song of thanksgiving that bears hope to the world. Amen. -Rev. Dana Werts

Notes:

DAILY DEVOTIONALS - WEEK SEVEN

SHARING YOUR STORY - LIFE INTERSECTIONS

DAY 4   **BE PERSERVERING - DON'T GIVE UP.**   **1 CORINTHIANS 13:7, MATTHEW 13:1-23**

"It [love] always protects, always trusts, always hopes, always perseveres." NIV *"Then he [Jesus] told them many things in parables, saying: 'A farmer went out to sow his seed. As he was scattering the seed, some fell along the path, and the birds came and ate it up. Some fell on rocky places, where it did not have much soil. It sprang up quickly, because the soil was shallow. But when the sun came up, the plants were scorched, and they withered because they had no root. Other seed fell among thorns, which grew up and choked the plants. Still other seed fell on good soil, where it produced a crop—a hundred, sixty or thirty times what was sown. Whoever has ears, let them hear.' The disciples came to him and asked, 'Why do you speak to the people in parables?' He replied, 'Because the knowledge of the secrets of the kingdom of heaven has been given to you, but not to them. Whoever has will be given more, and they will have an abundance. Whoever does not have, even what they have will be taken from them. This is why I speak to them in parables: Though seeing, they do not see; though hearing, they do not hear or understand. In them is fulfilled the prophecy of Isaiah: You will be ever hearing but never understanding; you will be ever seeing but never perceiving. For this people's heart has become calloused; they hardly hear with their ears, and they have closed their eyes. Otherwise they might see with their eyes, hear with their ears, understand with their hearts and turn, and I would heal them. But blessed are your eyes because they see, and your ears because they hear. For truly I tell you, many prophets and righteous people longed to see what you see but did not see it, and to hear what you hear but did not hear it. Listen then to what the parable of the sower means: When anyone hears the message about the kingdom and does not understand it, the evil one comes and snatches away what was sown in their heart. This is the seed sown along the path. The seed falling on rocky ground refers to someone who hears the Word and at once receives it with joy. But since they have no root, they last only a short time. When trouble or persecution comes because of the Word, they quickly fall away. The seed falling among the thorns refers to someone who hears the Word, but the worries of this life and the deceitfulness of wealth choke the Word, making it unfruitful. But the seed falling on good soil refers to someone who hears the Word and understands it. This is the one who produces a crop, yielding a hundred, sixty or thirty times what was sown.'"* NIV

What kind of farmer is this sower in the parable? If he knows that the seed will only grow in good soil, why not plant it there? Isn't that a waste to sow good seed in places it probably won't grow? Isn't that so like God? God's love is poured out on all, grace given freely, even if there is no guarantee of a harvest. God knows that some will fall into the hearts of those ready to respond. God's love never gives up on us.

There was a youth at the church who tried my patience, pushed my buttons, and hurt my feelings repeatedly. Yet, I could see below the surface, a beautiful girl, gifted to serve. I wanted to throw in the towel, more than once, but God's loud whisper in my soul was, "Keep loving her, don't give up on her." Some years later, she came to me and apologized for how difficult she had been to me. She was glad I never gave up on her. I rejoiced in knowing she was growing into her faith and using her gifts. God's love always protects, always trusts, always hopes, always perseveres.

Reflection: How can you scatter the seeds of God's love with no guarantee that someone will respond? Are you able to share your story with someone who rejects your words, and still continue to love them?

Prayer: Lord, thank you for never giving up on me. Enable me to love with your relentless love that gives with no expectation of return. Amen. -Rev. Dana Werts

Notes:

SHARING YOUR STORY - LIFE INTERSECTIONS

DAY 5　　　　　　**BE SIMPLE - LET YOUR LIGHT SHINE.**　　　　　**MATTHEW 5:14-16**

"You are the light of the world. A town built on a hill cannot be hidden. Neither do people light a lamp and put it under a bowl. Instead they put it on its stand, and it gives light to everyone in the house. In the same way, let your light shine before others, that they may see your good deeds and glorify your Father in heaven." NIV

Christian leaders sometimes like to use a lot of big "churchy" words, like sanctification, incarnation, and redemption when we preach and teach. Even words like glory and sin may not be clear to those who have not grown up in the church. Other Christians avoid sharing their faith because they feel inadequate to explain religion and believe they should leave these conversations for pastors. Jesus never used the word justification or atonement. He just told stories about sowing seeds and letting our light shine.

I was leading an after school program for middle school students in the community. Around Christmas, I had a nativity scene set up. One of the students asked me what that was about. I was caught off guard. There are some things we assume everyone understands. I started talking about the shepherds and the star, and then he picked up one of the wise men and said, "Is this God?" I realized that this student had no biblical background. I said a silent prayer and began to tell the story of Joseph and Mary. I shared Mary's encounter with the angel and that she became pregnant with God's son, Jesus. The boy rolled his eyes, and exclaimed, "And Joseph believed that story!"

Reflection: Are you able to share your personal faith stories with simple words and illustrations? If someone asked you who Jesus is, would you be able to share that in a way that was simple and understandable?

Prayer: Lord, enable me to share the story of your love in language that others can understand. You are always accessible to ordinary people. Let my words be simple, yet powerful expressions of your love. Amen. -Rev. Dana Werts

Notes:

DAILY DEVOTIONALS - WEEK SEVEN

SHARING YOUR STORY - LIFE INTERSECTIONS

DAY 6   **BE LOVING - IMITATE GOD.**   **EPHESIANS 5:1-2**

"Follow God's example, therefore, as dearly loved children and walk in the way of love, just as Christ loved us and gave himself up for us as a fragrant offering and sacrifice to God." NIV

The word "imitate" in Ephesians 5:1 is *mimetes* in the Greek, from which we also get our words: mime, imitation, and mimic. With no props or words, mime artists can convince you they are climbing a ladder, eating an apple, or other actions. Professional mime artists learn their moves by carefully observing and then copying exactly those actions. Jesus was the perfect mime of God. We are called to observe his actions carefully and do likewise, even offering our lives sacrificially.

I visited a friend who is well advanced in age, frail in body, and mostly confined to her home. Always active in service, she has been discouraged by her physical condition and asked, "What can I do now?" I reminded her that she can now devote her life to loving, which she is very gifted to do. Her words, her prayers, and her ability to make all who visit her feel loved is a holy service to God. When I leave my friend's home, the fragrance of Jesus lingers in my spirit.

Reflection: How can you imitate God in the example of Jesus in your encounters with others? Do your non-verbal actions reflect your internal faith? How can you live a life of love, rather than just a life of busy?

Prayer: Lord, let me remember how dearly loved I am as your child. Enable me to live my life with integrity, expressing my faith through loving actions. Transform me into the image of Christ. Amen.
-Rev. Dana Werts

Notes:

DAILY DEVOTIONALS - WEEK SEVEN

SHARING YOUR STORY - LIFE INTERSECTIONS

DAY 7   **BE PRAYING - BE READY TO TELL YOUR STORY.**   **COLOSSIANS 4:2-6**

"Devote yourselves to prayer, being watchful and thankful. And pray for us, too, that God may open a door for our message, so that we may proclaim the mystery of Christ, for which I am in chains. Pray that I may proclaim it clearly, as I should. Be wise in the way you act toward outsiders; make the most of every opportunity. Let your conversation be always full of grace, seasoned with salt, so that you may know how to answer everyone." NIV

In the intersections of the world, in our jobs, our neighborhoods, and our families, there are people who need to be invited to God's banquet of abundant life. We scatter the seed of God's love on everyone, shine our light into dark lives, and live a life of love. As we pray, we invite God to interrupt our lives with opportunities to share our God story and amazing things happen.

I missed my connection due to a mechanical problem with the plane and now had two hours to kill while I waited for the next flight. As I grumbled about this delay, I heard the song, "My Favorite Things" from the musical "The Sound of Music." I laughed, as I wasn't sure thinking of my favorite things would make everything better, but I prayed that God would use this delay for God's purposes. Much later, I boarded the plane, and a young soldier in uniform sat down next to me. As we took off, he started singing, "My Favorite Things" quietly. All I wanted to do was sleep on this late flight home, but the Spirit's alert was loud and clear. This was no coincidence. I took a chance and started a conversation with the young man. This led to a spiritual discussion about his life and a chance to share my God story.

Reflection: Have you prayed for opportunities to share your story? Are you willing to allow God to interrupt your life for a greater purpose?

Prayer: Lord, I pray that this day, you would use me for your purposes. Open my eyes to your divine appointments and give me the boldness to speak honestly in love. Amen. -Rev. Dana Werts

Notes:

SERMON OUTLINE - WEEK SEVEN

SHARING YOUR STORY - LIFE INTERSECTIONS

LUKE 14: 15-24, PSALM 107: 1-2 ☐NEW NIV☐

1. How do we stay "in-tune" with God?

    a. Our lives are multi-layered.

    b. We are complicated creatures.

    c. So often life in general is not easy.

2. In the midst of these multiple dimensions we see patterns of God's grace.

    a. These patterns of grace often come at life's intersections.

    b. They can only be seen if we are "in-tune" with God.

3. How do we become more in tune with God?

    a. One way is through recognizing and sharing our God stories.

        i. Psalm 107 reminds us to tell the story of God's faithfulness.

            1. Even the word faithfulness is multi-layered.

            2. The Hebrew word is *hesed (checed)* and it is often translated as the steadfast love of God.

            3. It can also be translated as loving kindness, steadfast love, mercy, and unfailing love.

        ii. So we hear these words from the psalmists: Tell of God's faithfulness, "Let the redeemed of the Lord" tell their story! (Note, it is only the new NIV that uses the word "story.")

4. We might begin with asking, who are the redeemed?

    a. Jesus himself tells a story about who these people are; sometimes the answer surprises us.

        i. When we hear Jesus' answer to the question of, "Who are the redeemed?" we can easily be shocked. Our parable today sheds some light on who these people might be.

            1. Initially, we can be shocked that people do not want to go to the banquet, they find a lot of excuses.

            2. Secondly, we can be shocked that Jesus invites those who do not "deserve" to enter into the banquet.

            3. Thirdly, we see that Jesus searches high and low for people whom he can invite to the banquet. (Go to the countryside.)

        ii. When we look closer, we see that we resemble this parable in more ways than we would like to admit

            1. First, we, too, are often "too busy."

                i. What are we too busy doing? Just like the list named by the banquet invitees, "I have to plant my field," "I just bought some oxen and I have to see if they are any good," "I just got married."

SERMON OUTLINE - WEEK SEVEN

    1. We can fill in our own excuses too.

        a. "My only morning of sleeping in is Sunday morning.: "I have two jobs, there is no free time..."

    2. What is the response of Jesus? Go invite others, anyone who will come.

    3. Search all over to find someone to come!

5. With whom do you identify in the story? The ones who refused to come? The ones who think they do not deserve to come?

    a. Share a story of being with those who might not think they deserved to come.

        i. Maybe this is a story of a mission trip.

        ii. Maybe this is a first-hand story of working with someone outside of your church walls.

    b. Maybe you do not identify with the ones who refused to come or the ones who did not think they deserved to come. Maybe you are the one giving the invitation? Maybe you are the servant?

6. We are going to pause for a minute and talk about the servants, the ones who are doing the inviting.

    a. That is one of the places that Jesus wants us to be, Jesus wants us to be the ones inviting and Jesus wants us to be sharing our stories. (Yes, we are to be as servants, the Bible uses the word servant time and time again to refer to followers of Christ.)

        i. Honestly, the other two options are categories we can fall into, but those are not places where we want to remain.

        ii. Refusing to come to the banquet or being among the ones who have not been invited yet is not the place of rest for followers of Christ.

    b. Perhaps the best place to be in this parable is to be the servant. The servant is the one Jesus sends to do the inviting.

    c. If we claim to be servants of the Lord, what are we to be doing? We are doing the inviting, right?

    d. Let the redeemed of the Lord tell the story!

    e. This is indeed a form of sharing our God stories, by inviting others to the banquet!

7. Over these past six weeks we have been sharing the how and where and when parts of telling our God stories, but the big part we have not talked about is why we share our God stories.

    a. Yes, we have shared the theological grounding: That Jesus commissions us to do so. (Matthew 28)

    b. We have shared the biblical thread that we have followed for these six weeks from the call of Abraham right through to Paul planting churches.

        i. There is another reason we share our God stories.

        ii. That reason is that something happens inside us when we are willing to step out in faith and share those stories.

        iii. What happens in us? Why do we share these stories?

            1. Because we grow with God.

SERMON OUTLINE - WEEK SEVEN

    2. Because we become part of something that is bigger than us.

    3. Because our hearts become malleable for God.

    4. Because sharing of our God stories helps us stay in tune with God!

8. If you think our lives are multi-layered, can we even imagine the multi-layers of God and of God's divine plan?

    a. God is not limited by space and time as we are, yet God invites us in.

    b. Our lives are so deeply connected with God's larger story, with the one who created us, redeemed us, and sustains us in life. God's larger plan is so much bigger than our individual lives, yet we all play a role in God's larger plan.

    c. How does God work through us? How do we have a life that is in-tune with God? What brings us to this "in-tune" place with God? How can God work through a malleable heart? How do the multiple dimensions of God's story fit into the multiple dimensions of our own stories?

9. It's all about God's grace.

    a. It's God's grace that sends the servants out to invite people to the banquet.

    b. It is God's grace that searches for all people, those whom others might have written off their lists, and Jesus says, "Come, there is a place for you."

10. This is how God's grace presents itself in our lives.

    a. John Wesley, founder of Methodism, would say there is one grace, which is a free, undeserved gift from God, like being invited to the banquet, but that grace or free gift presents itself in different ways.

        i. Prevenient - The grace that goes before us when we are unaware of God in our lives.

        ii. Convicting to the point of justification.

            1. This is the moment you realize that Jesus died for you and your sin on the cross.

            2. This is when you realize that if you were the only one on earth, Jesus still would have walked that path to Calvary, just for you.

        iii. Assurance of pardon. An assurance that there is something better beyond what we can see and know.

        iv. Finally, we move along the path of sanctification, growing with God.

            1. This sanctification is where the servants are.

            2. It is where the heart of the servant grows more and more in-tune with Jesus and what Jesus wants.

11. You might be saying, that is nice, but how does this tie into sharing my story?

    a. These are the multiple dimensions of God's story.

        i. Wherever we are in our walk with God, we have a story to tell.

            1. Whether you are not sure there is a God, or whether you are convinced that the second coming is coming tomorrow, wherever you are you have a story.

SERMON OUTLINE - WEEK SEVEN

    2. As people who are trying to be in relationship with God, God calls us to share that story with others.

    3. As we do so, we become part of something bigger.

    4. And as we do so, we also draw nearer to God ourselves, growing in what is called sanctification.

12. These are the patterns of grace we see in our own lives, and these are the same patterns we see in the lives of others.

    a. When we get ready to share a God story we can ask the Holy Spirit to reveal to us where that person is in their journey of grace:

        i. Are they totally unaware of God's grace? Then they fall under prevenient grace.

        ii. Have they just gotten involved in a church and they are ready to take an active role? Then they might have just accepted Christ into their lives and I might be able to connect with a part of my story when I realized that Jesus died for me?

        iii. Are they growing in faith, becoming more and more like Christ, and ready for next steps? Then they might be on the path of sanctification.

    b. Recognizing where someone else might be gives us a point of intersection in sharing a story of God's grace.

        i. These multiple dimensions of God's story intertwined with our stories give us a sense of purpose in beginning God conversations that will lead to deep and meaningful moments in life.

        ii. As we continue to share these God moments with others, we ourselves become more in-tune with God's desires. See, God continues to write your story too!

            1. So go, invite others to the banquet table.

            2. Let them know that there is room for all.

            3. And continue to share your God moments so that all may come to the feast!

Amen.

LITURGY FOR WORSHIP - WEEK SEVEN

SHARING YOUR STORY - LIFE INTERSECTIONS

FIRST SCRIPTURE READING: PSALM 107 1-3 (OR 1-32)

* * *Note* The new NIV uses the word *Story* in verse 2, old NIV does not nor does N SV. Check out the translations. *Let the redeemed of the Lo D tell their story.*

READING BEFORE THE SERMON: LUKE 14:15-24

Call to worship: (Based on Psalm 107 and Luke 14).

Give thanks to the Lord, for he is good; his love endures forever.
Let the redeemed of the Lord tell their story!
Gathered in this sacred space we desire to be your community of believers, ready to follow your lead.
Let the redeemed of the Lord tell their story!
Open our hearts, minds, and ears to hear your invitation to the heavenly banquet.
Let the redeemed of the Lord tell their story!
Empower us daily to share the heavenly banquet with others.
Blessed are the ones who feast at the banquet in the kingdom of God.

PRAYER OF CONFESSION:
God of the Heavenly Banquet: Too often you invite us to feast with you, and there are times when we are either not listening to hear the invitation, or we are too busy to stop and accept the invitation you offer. Forgive us we pray. In our haste and self-absorption we can also miss opportunities to invite others to feast at your table. Empower us by your Holy Spirit to see the outcasts and the disenfranchised with your eyes, knowing that we are each your created children, and we are all invited to your feast. Through the power of your Holy Spirit. Amen.

POSSIBLE HYMNS:
452   My Faith Looks Up to Thee
451   Be Thou My Vision
600   Wonderful Words of Life
707   Hymn of Promise
369   Blessed Assurance
569   We've a Story to Tell to the Nations
474   Precious Lord, take my hand
2071   Jesus name above all names.

* *Three digit page numbers refer to the United Methodist Hymnal*
* *Four digit page numbers refer to The Faith We Sing Hymnal*

POSSIBLE PRAISE SONGS:
Lifesong by Casting Crowns
One Thing Remains by Jesus Culture
Your Grace is Enough by Chris Tomlin
This is Amazing Grace by Phil Wickham
I Am a Friend of God by Israel Houghton
Your Love Never Fails by Jesus Culture

Bibliography

BIBLIOGRAPHY - BEST PRACTICES

Adeney, Frances S. *Graceful Evangelism: Christian Witness in a Complex World.* Grand Rapids, MI: Baker Academic, 2010.

Barna, George. *Re-Churching the Unchurched.* Ventura: Issachar Resource, 2000.

The Book of Discipline of the United Methodist Church, 2012. Nashville, TN: United Methodist Pub. House, 2012. Print.

Borden, Paul D. *Make or Break Your Church in 365 Days: A Daily Guide to Leading Effective Change.* Nashville, TN: Abingdon Press, 2012.

Bosch, David J. *Transforming Mission: Paradigm Shifts in Theology of Mission.* Maryknoll, NY: Orbis, 1991.

Chambers, Oswald, and James Reimann. *My Utmost for His Highest: An Updated Edition in Today's Language: The Golden Book of Oswald Chambers.* Grand Rapids, MI: Discovery House, 1992.

Coleman, Robert E. *The Master Plan of Evangelism.* Westwood, N.J: Revell, 1964.

Davis, Mark D. *Talking About Evangelism: A Congregational Resource; Holy Conversations.* Cleveland, OH: The Pilgrim Press, 2007.

Dawson, Scott. *Evangelism Today: Effectively Sharing the Gospel in a Rapidly Changing World.* Grand Rapids, MI: Baker Books, 2009.

Dowsett, R. *Dry Bones in the West,* in *Global Missiology for the 21st Century: Reflections from the Iguassu Dialogue,* ed. W. D. Taylor. Grand Rapids: Baker Academic, 2001.

Driscoll, James. *Sharing the Good News: A Workbook on Personal Evangelism.* D.Min. diss., Wesley Theological Seminary, 1996.

Driscoll, Mark. *The Radical Reformation: Reaching Out Without Selling Out.* Grand Rapids, MI: Zondervan, 2004.

Dunn, Dan W. *Offer Them Life: A Life-Based Evangelistic Vision.* Eugene, OR: Wipf & Stock, 2013.

Gortner, David. *Transforming Evangelism.* New York, NY: Church Publishing, 2008.

Hargraves, J. Stanley. *Telling The Story: The Gospel In Technological Age.* Macon, GA: Smyth & Helwys Publishing, Inc., 2009.

Hollinghurst, Steve. *Mission Shaped Evangelism: The Gospel in Contemporary Culture.* Norwich, UK: Canterbury Press, 2010.

Knight, Henry H. & F. Douglas Powe, Jr. *Transforming Evangelism: The Wesleyan Way of Sharing Faith.* Nashville, TN: Discipleship Resources, 2006.

Mittelberg, Mark. *Becoming Contagious Church: Increasing Your Church's Evangelistic Temperature.* Grand Rapids, MI: Zondervan, 2007.

Morrison, Timothy. *I Love To Tell the Story: Congregational Narrative in Evangelism.* DMin diss., Wesley Theological Seminary, 2011.

Packer, J. I. *Evangelism and the Sovereignty of God.* Downers Grove, IL: InterVarsity Press, 2008.

Pate, Stephen and Gene Wilkes. *Evangelism Where You Live: Engaging Your Community.* Saint Louis, MO: Chalice Press, 2008.

Pixner, Bargil. *With Jesus through Galilee According to the Fifth Gospel.* Collegeville, MN: Liturgical, 1996.

BIBLIOGRAPHY - BEST PRACTICES

Posterski, Donald C. *Reinventing Evangelism: New Strategies for Presenting Christ in Today's World.* Downers Grove, IL: InterVarsity Press, 1989.

Powe, F. Douglas, Jr. *New Wine New Wineskins: How African American Congregations Can Reach New Generations.* Nashville, TN: Abingdon Press, 2012.

Quicke, Michael J. *360-Degree Leadership: Preaching to Transform Congregations.* Grand Rapids, MI: Baker Publishing Group, 2006.

Roxburgh, Alan J. and Fred Romanuk, *The Missional Leader; Equipping Your Church To Reach Changing World.* San Francisco: Wiley Imprint, Jossey-Bass, 2006.

Scharen, Christian. *Faith as Way of Life: A Vision of Pastoral Leadership.* Grand Rapids, MI: William B. Eerdmans Publishing Company, 2008.

Sensing, Tim. *Qualitative Research: A Multi-Methods Approach to Projects for a Doctor of Ministry Theses.* Eugene, OR: Wipf & Stock, 2011.

Stone, Bryan. *Evangelism after Christendom: The Theology and Practice of Christian Witness.* Grand Rapids, MI: Brazo Press, 2007.

Sweet, Leonard. *Post-Modern Pilgrims: First Century Passion for the 21st Century World.* Tenessee: Broadman and Holman, 2000.

Tenny-Brittian, Bill. *Hitchhiker's Guide to Evangelism.* Saint Louis, MO: Chalice Press, 2008.

United Methodist Hymnal. Nashville, TN: The United Methodist Publishing House, 1989.

Wesley, John. *The Works of John Wesley Volume 18, Journals and Diaries I, (1735-1738),* edited by W. Reginald Ward and Richard P. Heitzenrater. Nashville, TN: Abingdon Press, 1988.

Woodward, J.R. *Creating a Missional Culture: Equipping the Church for the Sake of the World.* Westmont, IL: IVP books, 2012.

BIBLIOGRAPHY - THEOLOGICAL

Birch, Bruce C. *A Theological Introduction to the Old Testament*. Nashville: Abingdon, 1999.

Byrne, Brendan, S.J. *Inheriting the Earth: The Pauline Basis of a Spirituality for Our Time*. New York, NY: Alba House, Society of St. Paul, 1965.

Chester, Tim and Steve Timmis. *Total Church. A Radical Reshaping around Gospel and Community*. Wheaton, IL: Crossway Publishing, 2008.

Ehrensperger, Kathy. *Paul At The Crossroads of Cultures: Theologizing in the Space Between*. New York, NY: Bloomsbury, 2013.

Gallagher, Robert L. and Paul Hertig, editors. *Mission in Acts: Ancient Narratives in Contemporary Context*. Maryknoll, NY: Orbis Books, 2004.

Georgi, Dieter, Translated by David E. Green. *Theocracy: In Paul's Praxis and Theology*. Minneapolis, MN: Fortress Press, 1991.

Gonzalez, Justo L. *Essential Theological Terms*, Louisville, KY: Westminster John Knox Press, 2005.

Guton, Colin. *The Community, The Trinity and The Being of the Church*, Edinburgh: T&T Clark, 2001.

Harding, Mark and Alanna Nobbs, editors. *All Things to All Cultures: Paul Among Jews, Greeks, and Romans*. Grand Rapids, MI: William B. Eerdman Publishing Company, 2013.

Harrison, Nonna Verna. *Human Community as an Image of the Holy Trinity*, St. Vladimir's Theological Quarterly, 2005.

Hays, Richard B. *The Faith of Jesus Christ: The Narrative Substructure of Galatians 3:1-4:11, Second Edition*. Dearborn, MI: William B. Eerdmann Publishing Company, 1983.

Hood, Roger, and Carolyn Hoyle. *A Worldwide Perspective*. Oxford: Oxford University Press, 2008.

Johnson, Luke Timothy. *The Creed: What Christians Believe and Why It Matters*, New York: Image/ Doubleday Press, 2003.

Martin, Robert K. *Transforming Communities Into Communion*, Draft 2013.

Murphy-O'Connor, Jerome. *St. Paul's Corinth: Text and Archaeology*. Collegeville, MN: The Liturgical Press, 2002.

Newbigin, Leslie. *The Open Secret: An Introduction to the Theology of Mission*. London: SPCK, 1995.

Sanders, E. P. *Paul: A Very Short Introduction*. Oxford, UK; New York, NY: Oxford University Press, 2001.

___*Paul and Palestinian Judaism: A Comparison of Patterns of Religion*. Philadelphia, PA: Fortress Press, 1977.

Skinner, Matthew L. *Locating Paul: Places of Custody as Narrative Settings in Acts 21 - 28*. Atlanta, GA: Society of Biblical Literature, 2003.

Soards, Marion L. *The Speeches in Acts: Their Content, Context, and Concern*. Louisville, KY: Westminster/John Knox Press, 1994.

Thiselton, Anthony C. *The Living Paul: An Introduction to the Apostle's Life and Thought*. Downers Grove, IL: InterVarsity Press, 2009.

Ware, James. *The Mission of the Church in Paul's Letter to the Philippians in the Context of Ancient Judaism*. Koninklijke, The Netherlands: Brill Academic Publishing, 2005.

Wright, N.T. *Paul and the Faithfulness of God: Book I, Parts I & II*. Minneapolis, MN: Fortress Press, 2013.

BIBLIOGRAPHY - THEOLOGICAL

___*Paul and the Faithfulness of God: Book II, Parts III & IV.* Minneapolis, MN: Fortress Press, 2013.

___Wright, N.T. *Justification: God's Plan & Paul's Vision.* Downers Grove, IL: IVP Academic, 2009.

___Wright, N. T. *Surprised by Scripture: Engaging Contemporary Issues.* New York, NY: Harper Collins, 2014.

BIBLIOGRAPHY - INTERNET

http://www.biblesearchers.com/yahshua/beithillel/beitshammai.shtml, accessed October 2, 2015.

http://www.thegospelcoalition.org/article/factchecker-misquoting-francis-of-assisi, accessed September 18, 2015.

https://www.quora.com/Who-are-the-top-5-most-respected-and-influential-New-Testament- scholars-today, n.d., accessed September 29, 2015.

Mohler, R. Albert, Jr. *Moralistic Therapeutic Deism—The New American Religion,* April 18, 2005. http://www.christianpost.com/news/6266/#ivzM6qSBwpctuWgP.99, accessed November 26, 2015.

Towers Watson. "UMC Call to Action Report: Vital Congregations Research Project, accessed June 12, 2015.

Findings Report for Steering Team, June 2010. http://umccalltoaction.org/files/CTA_TOWERS WATSON_RPTS_45-126.pdf, accessed January 12, 2015.

Vital Statistics, http://vitalsigns.trendsendapp.com/reports/25/overview/daterange/2013-01-01-2013-12-31/filter/26396, accessed January 13, 2015.

Wikipedia. https://en.wikipedia.org/wiki/Postchristianity, accessed August 22, 2015.

Wright, N. T., On Justification - Al Mohler, Brian Vickers, Denny Burk, Mark Seifrid, Tom Schreiner. *YouTube.* YouTube, n.d. Web., accessed 14 Sept. 2015. https://www.youtube.com/watch?v=tA-2PjalU6E.

Wright, N. T. Book of Romans, part one of ten, *YouTube.* YouTube, n.d. Web., accessed 18 September 2015. https://www.youtube.com/watch?v=M8WwFmUmEFo.

Wright, N. T., What Paul Really Said, *YouTube.* YouTube, n.d. Web., accessed 29 September 2015, https://www.youtube.com/watch?v=aDC_EUfV1b8.

Wright, N. T., Paul and the Faithfulness of God (University of Edinburgh). *YouTube.* YouTube, n.d. Web., accessed September 14, 2015. https://www.youtube.com/watch?v=0XszYFTkpGo.

DEVOTIONAL WRITERS AND CONTRIBUTORS

Lance Barb is a member of Brook Hill United Methodist Church, in Frederick, Maryland, and has shared a powerful witness of a God Story.

Rev. Dr. Michelle Holmes Chaney is a Full Elder of the Baltimore Washington Conference of the United Methodist Church. She currently serves at Centreville United Methodist Church in Northern Virginia. She received her Doctorate degree from Wesley Theological Seminary.

Andy and Melissa Cimbala, currently serve as campus leaders for DiscipleMakers at Shippensburg University. DiscipleMakers is a Christian campus ministry based in Pennsylvania with the goal of raising up the next generation of leaders for the Church by training college students in Bible study, gospel-driven discipleship, and evangelism.

*Rev. Sherri Comer-*Cox is an Elder in the Baltimore Washington Conference of the United Methodist Church. She received her Master of Divinity from Wesley Theological Seminary and currently serves at Taylorsville United Methodist Church.

Rev. Dr. Wanda Bynum Duckett wrote the poem, "I Am Mission" used in chapter four. She is a Full Elder of the Baltimore Washington Conference of the United Methodist Church. She received her Doctorate of Ministry from Wesley Theological Seminary, and currently serves as the District Superintendent of the Baltimore Metro District.

Rev. Rodney Hudson is a Full Elder in the Baltimore Washington Conference of the United Methodist Church. He received his M. Div. from Virginia Union Theological Seminary and is currently serving at Ames United Methodist Church. His words of witness were used in the sermon outline in chapter four.

Rev. Dr. Wade Martin, a Full Elder of the Baltimore Washington Conference of the United Methodist Church, currently serving at Brook Hill United Methodist Church. He received his Doctorate of Ministry from Wesley Theological Seminary in church leadership.

Rev. Dana Werts is a Full Elder in the Baltimore Washington Conference of the United Methodist Church. She received her Master of Divinity from Wesley Theological Seminary and currently serves as Associate Pastor at Brook Hill United Methodist Church.

Pastor Lynn Wilson is a licensed local pastor in the Baltimore Washington Conference and completed her Course of Study requirements at Wesley Theological Seminary. She currently serves Calvary United Methodist Church in Martinsburg, W.V.

Author's Note

The purpose of this project was to teach and empower faith based people to know their God stories, to be able to articulate their God stories, and to have a desire to share their faith narratives in order that others might become disciples of Jesus Christ, and in order to advance God's divine story of ushering in the kingdom of God. May you be empowered by the Holy Spirit with a renewed sense of purpose for your life, and may you have and seize opportunities to share your God stories. May it be so - Amen.

-Rev. Dr. Sarah B. Dorrance

I pray that you will go forth and share your God story.

Amen

About the Author
Sarah B. Dorrance

Pastor Sarah is the lead pastor at Middletown United Methodist Church in Middletown, Maryland, and an ordained elder in the Baltimore Washington Conference of the United Methodist Church. She is also an ICF Certified Coach, and served part-time as resource staff on the Western Region of the BWC where she assisted in coaching ordained pastors. In addition to this book series, she is the author of several articles found in Leading Ideas from the Lewis Center for Church Leadership, and a co-author of *Reclaiming the Wesleyan Tradition: John Wesley's Sermons for Today.* She is the proud mother of two adult daughters and their husbands as well as three grandchildren. She is a member of the Columbia Orchestra for which she plays the French Horn. In her free time, she enjoys hiking, biking, and kayaking. Her deepest desire is for everyone to hear the Gospel message, and know that Jesus loves them.

To learn more about Pastor Sarah, visit her websites at
www.revsarahdorrance.wordpress.com
or www.sarahdorrance.com.